UNFINISHED BUSINESS

KEN HUDNALL
And
SHARON HUDNALL
OMEGA PRESS
EL PASO, TEXAS

UNFINISHED BUSINESS

COPYRIGHT © 2019 KEN HUDNALL

All rights reserved. No part of the book may be reproduced or transmitted in any form or by any means, graphic, electronic, or mechanical, including photocopying, recording, taping or by any information storage or retrieval system, without the permission in writing of the author.

OMEGA PRESS

http://www.kenhudnall.com

FIRST EDITION

Printed in the United States of America

OTHER WORKS BY THE SAME AUTHOR UNDER THE NAME KEN HUDNALL FROM OMEGA PRESS

MANHATTAN CONSPIRACY SERIES
Blood on the Apple
Capitol Crimes
Angel of Death
Confrontation

THE OCCULT CONNECTION
UFOs, Secret Societies and Ancient Gods
The Hidden Race
Flying Saucers
UFOs and the Supernatural
UFOs and Secret Societies
UFOs and Ancient Gods
Evidence of Alien Contact
Secrets of Dulce
Unidentified Flying Objects
Sensual Alien Encounters
Strange Creatures from Time and Space
Beyond Roswell
Alien Encounters
Mysteries of Space
Battle of Los Angeles
Is Someone On The Moon?
Intervention
Mystery Men

DARKNESS
When Darkness Falls
Fear the Darkness

SPIRITS OF THE BORDER
(with Connie Wang)
The History and Mystery of El Paso Del Norte

The History and Mystery of Fort Bliss, Texas
(with Sharon Hudnall)
The History and Mystery of the Rio Grande
The History and Mystery of New Mexico
The History and Mystery of the Lone Star State
The History and Mystery of Arizona
The History and Mystery of Tombstone, AZ
The History and Mystery of Colorado
Echoes of the Past
El Paso: A City of Secrets
Tales From the Nightshift
The History and Mystery of Sin City
The History and Mystery of Concordia
The History and Mystery of ASARCO
Military Ghosts
School Spirits
Restless spirits
Railroad Ghosts
Nautical Ghosts
Haunted Hotels
Haunted Hotels in Arizona and Colorado
Ghosts of Albuquerque
The History and Mystery of Tucson
The History and Mystery of Santa Fe

SHADOW WARS
The Shadow Rulers
The Secret Elite

THE ESTATE SALE MURDERS
Dead Man's Diary
A Bloody Afternoon of Fun

BOOK OF SECRETS
Ancient Secrets
Secrets of the Dark Web

Northwood Conspiracy

No Safe Haven: Homeland Insecurity

Where No Car Has Gone Before

Seventy Years and No Losses: The History of the Sun Bowl

How Not To Get Published

Lost Cities and Hidden Tunnels Along the Border

Vampires, Werewolves and Things That Go Bump in The Night

Border Escapades of Billy the Kid

Criminal law for the Layman

Understanding Business Law

Language of the Law

Death of Innocence: The Life and Death of Vince Foster

The Veterans' Practice Primer

Why Would They Say It?

PUBLISHED BY PAJA BOOKS
The Occult Connection: Unidentified Flying Objects

PUBLISHED BY PRUNE DANISH PRESS
Why Would They Say It?

DEDICATION

As with all of my endeavors, this would not be possible without the support and assistance of my lovely wife, Sharon Hudnall.

TABLE OF CONTENTS

CHAPTER ONE 11
WHAT UNFINISHED BUSINESS? 11

CHAPTER TWO 17
JACK THE AXEMAN 17

CHAPTER THREE 53
THE BEAUTIFUL CIGAR GIRL 53

CHAPTER FOUR 63
THE VILLISCA AXE MURDERS 63

CHAPTER FIVE 77
THE MURDER OF MARY PHAGAN 77

CHAPTER SIX 137
THE MURDER OF NORA FULLER 137

CHAPTER SEVEN **151**

THE DEATH OF LITLE LORD FAUNTLEROY **151**

CHAPTER EIGHT **155**

THE ATLANTA RIPPER **155**

CHAPTER NINE **173**

THE MURDER OF PAT GARRETT **173**

CHAPTER TEN **183**

THE MURDER OF WILLIAM DESMOND TAYLOR **183**

CHAPTER ELEVEN **197**

THE CAMDEN TOWN MURDER **197**

INDEX **213**

CHAPTER ONE
WHAT UNFINISHED BUSINESS?

What unfinished business could we be talking about here? Well, it seems that as a result of today's crime solving television shows, most people believe that through the use of science, every crime can be solved in 60 minutes, taking time out for commercials. But this is not true and has not been true, though through the use of modern DNA techniques, more and more cases are being solved that every before. It has become the rule for most police departments that cold cases are being pulled out of dusty filing cabinets and the evidence is being given a new review using current scientific processes. But what about those who are really cold cases, say those that are a hundred years old or more? Can modern techniques work on cases as old as these?

Our crime scene investigators are, for the most part, scientists and specialists in their own right, each trained to thoroughly investigate certain piece or type of evidence. However, some aspect of criminal investigation that are standard today were not even thought of a hundred years ago.

Crime scene investigation, today, consists of lifting fingerprints and looking for DNA evidence, but this is a result of relatively recent scientific discoveries. As an example, the Chinese have been using fingerprints as a means for identification, authentication and verification since before the 3rd century BC. However, the first use of a fingerprint on a contract in the British Empire was in July of 1858 in Jungipoor in India when the local chief magistrate asked a native business man to place his fingerprints on a contract.

It was not until July of 1877 that American Thomas Taylor proposed that finger and palm prints left on any object might be used to solve crimes. The first known usage of fingerprints in the United States was in 1882 when Gilbert Thompson of the U.S. Geological Survey in New Mexico used his own thumb print on a document to help prevent forgery.

Then of course, there was Alphonse Bertillon, a clerk in the Prefecture of Police in Paris, France who, in 1882, developed a system of classification known as anthropometry using measurements of various body parts. Widespread usage of his system began in 1888. He also instituted the use of fingerprints, but only as an assist to this own system known as the Bertillon Method.

The first use of fingerprints in this country began in 1903 in New York City when two individuals in Leavenworth Penitentiary turned out to have the same Bertillon Measurements. Fingerprints were found to be more useful in identifying who was who in this case. So, it is clear that it was not until after the beginning of the 20th century that fingerprints were even looked at as a major method of identification. So how were investigators to track down a faceless killer without the most basic tools that we take for granted today?

DNA profiling has become the subject of hundreds of television crime dramas, but in spite of such exposure, it has not been allowed in forensic investigations for all that long. DNA profiling was first primarily used to determine paternity, but it was found that it had other uses in the investigative field. It was first used in the court system in 1986 when police in England asked a molecular biologist by the name of Alec Jefferies, who had been investigating the use of DNA for forensic investigation to use DNA to verify the confession of a 17-year old boy to committing two rape murders in the England Midlands. The test proved that the teenager was in fact not telling the truth and the actual attacker was caught, also using DNA testing.

We are aware of a few of the unique murder cases from the 1800s and the early 1900s such as Jack the Ripper, who terrorized London during the heady days of the Victorian era, but few are aware of some of the unbelievably monstrous cases that happened in this country during the waning years of the 19th century and the early years of the 20th century.

So, in the next chapters, let us look at some of the major unsolved cases of 100 years ago and see if it is possible to use today's scientific methods to solve these cases. Let us try to clean up some unfinished business.

CHAPTER TWO
JACK THE AXEMAN

Murders are difficult to solve when there is clear motive and a known suspect. However, when there is absolutely no motive and there is not even an inkling of an idea as to whom the suspect might be, solving a murder is almost impossible,

Everyone has heard of the infamous Jack the Ripper[1], the name given to an unidentified serial killer who terrorized the Whitechapel section of London in 1888. The Whitechapel area of London in the 1880s was somewhat a world unto itself, with its overcrowding, terrible work and living conditions. Even the very atmosphere of the area aided

---

[1] He was also called the Whitechapel Murderer as well as Leather Apron.

the actions of this mysterious killer, who slipped through the rainy, foggy London nights prowling through the winding dingy streets to ambush his next victim.

Though most writers claim that Jack the Ripper killed only the five best known prostitutes liked to him by popular legend there were actually eleven or more murders actually linked to him by the police[2], there is evidence that he may have killed several more than reported before vanishing into the mists and fog of London. All of these associated murders demonstrated the same modus operandi that became known as the ripper's trademark, throats slashed, abdominal and genital area mutilation, removal of internal organs and facial mutilations.

Just as today, in the mid 1800s London was receiving a major influx of immigrants from numerous other countries that swelled the population of London beyond belief. Whether it was immigrants from Ireland or Jewish refugees

---

[2] The local police called these killings the Whitechapel Murders

escaping the pogroms in Tsarist Russia, these new comers, mostly poor, some with just the clothes on their backs, swelled the population of the poorer neighborhoods almost to the bursting point. It was from these struggling immigrants that poured into the ever-growing slums that Jack the Ripper chose his victims, committing increasingly gruesome murders until he inexplicably vanished into history – or did he?

Across the ocean, the New Orleans, Louisiana of the early 1900s is almost a world unto itself. Though it is a major city of the southern United States, it is, and has always been, unlike any other city in the country primarily due to its French Cajun roots. The French Quarter has long been known as an area where dreams are born, and one can lose oneself in the sounds of music that can be heard few other places.

There is also an aura of mystery and delicious danger that overlies this city as practitioners of voodoo and the other black arts work side by side with those who strive to modernize this steadily growing city. New Orleans was the home of the mysterious and lovely Marie Laveau, called the Queen of Voodoo who held the entire city in the palm of one delicate hand for several decades.

As a major coastal city, New Orleans also boasts an atmosphere unlike few other locations. The night can range from hot and sultry to cool and moist as your skin is caressed by cool ocean breezes if you are lucky enough to live close to the shore, or hot and muggy in the winding streets of the growing city. In short, it is literally unlike any place else and that may well have been part of the reason that New Orleans had its own mystery killer, who, interestingly enough chose his victims from among the more prosperous Italian immigrants.

Was it simply a coincidence that Jack the Axeman, as many came to call this mysterious killer, chose his victims from among those who came to this country seeking a better life? Most believe he killed only Italian grocers, but in actuality, he killed individuals form other professions as well. Even more interesting was the reaction of neighbors who wanted to get involved in these tragedies. These murders gave neighbors and victims the change to settle scores, real or imagined, with those unfortunate enough to get caught up in the tragedy as well. And of course, there was the media, fanning the flames, accusing, trying and convicting those suspected of being the culprits in the newspapers without any more evidence than the police had.

Like the killings attributed to Jack the Ripper, the first killing by Jack the Axeman raised the eyebrows of the victims' social set, but it did not provoke the fear that the additional murders would cause later. It should be considered that the backdrop for these murders was There was also a world war raging in Europe in 1918 and a lot of American soldiers were there, as a result most of the attention of not only the city but the world was focused on the war news. In the beginning, more attention was paid to the war news that to the news closer to home.

THE FIRST ATTACK

What would become a reign of terror in this city caught between two worlds, as it were, began on the night of May 23, 1918. In the early hours of May 24, Joseph and Catherine Maggio, an Italian immigrant couple who ran a small grocery were discovered in their beds, dead. They had been assaulted with their own axe which had been taken from their own backyard. Their throats had also been sliced with a razor. In fact, Mrs. Maggio's throat had been slashed so deeply that her head was almost severed form her body. The killer left the razor lying on the floor in a pool of blood.

Subsequent investigation revealed that nothing appeared to have been stolen. Beneath Mr. Maggio's pillow was over a hundred dollars in cash from his store. The killer, who also ignored Mrs. Maggio's jewelry lying on a dresser, had apparently entered and left the combination home/store by chiseling out a panel from the rear door.

In another similarity to the Ripper case, a handwritten message was found written on the sidewalk near the Maggio's home - "*Mrs. Maggio is going to sit up tonight just like Mrs. Toney.*" It was never discovered who had written the message.

In their enthusiasm to quickly close the case and based on the unsupported word of a neighbor that he had seen Andrew Maggio, Joseph's brother, come home between two and three in the morning, both Andrew and Jake, Maggio's brothers who also lived in the combination home/business were arrested on literally no evidence other than living in the same house. Both were shortly released.

Long time members of the police force, and some reporters to be sure, remembered that in 1911, three other Italian grocers had been murdered by an axe wielding killer. In two of the cases, their wives had also been murdered. The victims were identified as Cruti, Rosetti and Tony Schiambra[3]. There were those who thought that the Mrs. Toney in the message found on the sidewalk referred to Tony Schiambra's wife. These cases were never solved as well.

It should be noted that there were a number of problems with the investigation of this case. The detective placed in charge of the Maggio case was killed by a burglary suspect. So, a new lead detective had to be assigned who was unable to find the numerous leads mentioned to the press by his predecessor.

THE SECOND ATTACK

Such were the barrage of lurid headlines from the battlefields of France that filled the front pages of the local papers that by the time of the second attack, most people had forgotten about the first attack.

---

[3] More recent research has failed to find any killings of victims by these names.

In June of 1918, a Polish Immigrant by the name of Louis Besumer, and his paramour, Harriet Lowe[4], were attacked in their bed with an axe taken from their yard by a mysterious killer. Just as in the first killing, a panel had been removed from the door to allow the killer to enter and once again, nothing was stolen from with the home or the business. The victims had their throats slashed and their faces were mutilated, though whether intentionally or as a result of the attack was uncertain. However, in this instance, both of the victims survived the attack, though Harriet Lowe died of her injuries later.

Lowe's behavior was odd, to say the least. Though she professed not to know the identity of her assailant, Lowe first accused Besumer of trying to kill her and then said that he was a German spy. The District Attorney, under intense pressure to solve the axe murders, based on what he called a

---

[4] It was hard to know if the neighbors were more shocked to find that the couple were living in sin or that there had been an attack.

death bed statement by Lowe, ignoring the similarities between this attack and the Maggio murders, charged Besumer with the murder of Lowe when she died two months after the attack. While he did not accuse Besumer of the earlier murder of the Maggio's, he certainly did nothing to discourage such talk among the citizens of New Orleans.

Unfortunately, for the District Attorney, charging Besumer with the murder of Lowe did not stop the real Jack the Axeman. Though the DA brought Besumer to trial for the murder of Lowe, Besumer was acquitted, leaving the DA with egg on his face. There had been a rumor that the Mafia was involved in the Maggio killings since they were Italian, but since Besumer was not Italian, this line of inquiry fell short.

On its face, the Besumer case seemed tied to the Maggio murders. The first witness, John Zanca arrived at the Besumer's grocery in the early hours of June 28, 1918 to deliver bread and cakes. He found that a panel of the door had been carved out, so he pounded on the door until a groggy Louis Besumer, blood streaming from a bloody head wound answered the door. Zanca pushed past him and discovered Lowe in her bed with a very bloody wound to her head.

While in the hospital, Harriet Lowe made the statements about Besumer being a German spy which brought in the federal involvement. He was later cleared of being a spy. It should be understood that the only evidence ever submitted that Besumer was guilty of anything were Lowe's completely unsupported statements.

Harriet Lowe also began to talk about the attacks. She said that Besumer was sitting at a desk working on his accounts while she went into the kitchen. According to her story it was while she was checking on some prunes, she had been cooking that she blacked out. She believed that she had been attacked in the kitchen and then her body was oved as she remembered nothing of the attack nor going to bed. Then she said, in spite of not remembering going to bed, she remembered waking up in the bed and seeing s man standing over her, making some sort of motions with his hands. Then she saw the axe. At this point, she said, she screamed.

She gave a brief description of the man she saw standing over her bed. She said he was tall and heavy-set. She also was certain he was a white man, with dark brown hair that almost stood on end. He was wearing a white shirt, opened at the neck. The next thing she remembers was waking up on the gallery with her face in a pool of blood.

Of course, in the next interview, her story changed in several major respects. In spite of the continually changing narrative, the Police dutifully followed up on every allegation she made, to include one that it was Besumer that had tried to kill her. How much of these changes were due to the urging of the police and how much were based on her inability to think clearly after the head injuries was never discussed.

Based entirely on her statements, with some relief, police officials decided that the Besumer case was not an Axeman attack, but that Besumer himself had inflicted his own wounds in order to coverup trying to kill Harriett Lowe. It must be remembered that this was before the age of forensic science when a policeman's gut feelings solved cases whether they were correct or not was not a concern. Closing cases, especially high-profile cases, was the order of the day, especially in regard to the Axeman. Unfortunately, the jury did not agree with them.

There were a few other interesting tidbits that came to light about the Besumer case. Harriet Lowe became the center of a media circus, as she continually made scandalous and often false statements relating to both the attacks and the character of Louis Besumer. The *Times-Picayune* sensationalized Lowe and her outspoken nature upon discovering that she was not the wife of Besumer, but his mistress. A Charity Hospital source discovered the scandal, when Besumer asked to be directed to the room of "Mrs. Harriet Lowe," and was inevitably denied access as no woman by that name was a patient. Besumer's legal wife arrived from Cincinnati in the days immediately following the discovery, which further inflamed the ongoing drama.

Lowe further gained media attention as she repeatedly made statements which voiced her dislike of the New Orleans chief of police, as well as her reluctance to comply with police questioning. After the truth of her marital status was revealed publicly, Lowe told reporters from the Times-Picayune that she would no longer aid the police in their investigation, as she suspected that it had been Chief Mooney who first informed the press of the scandal.

Despite the scandal, and her delirious statements which suggested that Besumer was a German spy, Lowe returned to the home she shared with Besumer weeks after the attack. One side of her face was partially paralyzed due to the severity of the attack. Lowe died August 5, 1918, just two days after doctors performed surgery in an effort to repair her partially paralyzed face. Just prior to her death, Lowe told authorities that she suspected it was Louis Besumer who had attacked her. Besumer spent nine months in jail before being released by a jury that took only ten minutes to reach a verdict. The investigation was so botched the two lead investigators were demoted.

THE THIRD ATTACK

Over the next fourteen months, Jack the Axeman[5] added a number of names to his list of victims. On August 5, 1918, coincidentally the same day that Harriet Lowe died in Charity Hospital after a failed surgery, the mystery killer attacked 28-year-old Anna Schneider, also known as Mrs. Edward Schneider, who survived but was unable to identify her attacker.

She reported that she awoke to find a dark figure standing over her just as he bashed her in the head

---

[5] As in the Whitechapel Murders, the name came from the Press.

repeatedly. Her scalp was torn open and she bleed freely. She was not discovered until sometime after midnight when her husband, who had worked late came home. Interestingly enough, in this the Axeman changed his methods somewhat. In the Schneider case, there was no door panel chiseled out, instead, he, or perhaps she, came in through an open window. Additionally, the police never found an axe, leaving all to wonder what weapon was used for the attack. But as usual, nothing was stolen.

Frankly, the failure of the Axeman to kill Mrs. Schneider was somewhat surprising as she was nine months pregnant at the time of the attack. Her head of bashed and she was bleeding horribly, but she made a full recovery and only a week after the attack, gave birth to a healthy baby.

When questioned, Mrs. Schneider could remember nothing about the attack. She was just happy to be alive. If anything, the deviation from the Axeman's modus operandi should have raised questions about whether this was a related attack, but it did not.

Her husband told police that nothing was stolen from the home, besides six or seven dollars that had been in his wallet. The windows and doors of the apartment appear to have not been forced open, and authorities came to the conclusion that the woman was most likely attacked with a lamp that had been on a nearby table.

James Gleason, who police said was an ex-convict, was arrested shortly after Schneider was found. Gleason was later released due to a complete lack of evidence and stated that he originally ran from authorities because he had so often been arrested. Lead investigators began to publicly speculate that the attack was related to the previous incidents involving Besumer and Maggio.

THE FOURTH ATTACK

Due to the delay between the first and second attacks, no one really expected another attack almost immediately.

On August 10, 1918, Joseph Romano, an elderly man who earned his living as a barber, not a grocer, though he was Italian, was attacked while sleeping in his bed and died at Charity Hospital.

In this case, also sleeping in the house were Joseph's two nieces, Pauline, aged 18 and Mary, aged 13. Though both girls were wakened by sounds coming from their uncle's room, only Pauline investigated. Mary saw nothing but screamed just the same since her sister's screams had scared her.

Pauline later testified that the two girls heard noises coming from their uncle's room and Pauline opened the connecting door to see a tall, dark, heavy-set man wearing a dark suit and a black slouch hat standing by her uncle's bed. She claimed that she was also unable to tell if the mystery man was black or white, though she thought maybe he had been white. And said that he had vanished as if he had wings.

As is the case in regard to many witness statements, over the weeks after witnesses the attack on her uncle, Pauline talked to many reporters and began to remember many things she could not possibly have known. Additionally, some of the early statements she reported were decidedly odd.

For example, she said that when she opened the door and saw the man standing over her uncle, she screamed, and the mystery man seemed to literally vanish. Then her uncle, who staggered out of bed, stumbled into the parlor and said, "I have been hit, I don't know who did it. Call the Charity Hospital." Joseph Romano was said to have walked to the ambulance but later died at the hospital

According to the police, this attack had all of the signs expected form an Axeman attack. There was a panel chiseled out of the rear door and there was a bloody axe found in the backyard of the Romano home. Once again, though there was money in Romano's bedroom, nothing was taken.

Of course, even though the police now had at least two bloody axes in evidence, no one even thought about the possibility of taking fingerprints. Such things just were not done back then. Then two, since there was no central file of fingerprints against which to check the ones that might have been taken form the axes, what good would they have been? No, this case was going to be solved the old-fashioned way, with shoe leather and gut feelings.

This fourth attack also brought out a wave of hysteria that literally swept over the immigrant neighborhood. Men began to arm themselves to protect their families and stayed on guard at night. Strangers were viewed with great suspicion, of course, no one could be sure that the Axeman was really a stranger or perhaps someone from the neighborhood who had literally lost his or her mind.

The news of the Romano attack also had the result that brought out a number of previously unreported incidents that may or may not have been relevant. As with any crime of this magnitude, everyone wanted to both distance themselves from the mayhem, but at the same time, get their fifteen minutes of fame by helping to solve it.

Al Durand, another grocer reported finding an axe and a chisel outside his backdoor on the morning of August 11. Another grocer, Joseph LeBeouf, who lived only a block from the Romano's home reported finding that someone had chiseled a panel out of his rear door on July 28th, he also reported finding an axe lying in the backyard. It seemed that everyone had a story about the Axeman.

THE FIFTH ATTACK

Between the fourth attack and the fifth attack, some seven months lapsed causing the citizens of New Orleans to breathe a sigh of relief. The smart money said the killer had run his course in the area or been arrested for some other charge or perhaps killed and it was never reported. Whatever may have been the reason for the lull in the attacks, it was thought by some and hoped by many that the attacks were over.

However, on March 10, 1919, the mysterious Axeman entered the home of the Cortimiglias and attacked father Charles, Mother Rosie and their daughter Mary. Charles and Rose survived, but Mary died.

In the midst of mourning her dead child, Rosie Cortimiglia accused numerous people of being the killer before she finally accused two neighbors, Iorlando Jordano and his son Frank Jordano, of being the ones that broke into her bedroom and attacked her husband herself and her child.

Even though her husband testified that the two accused neighbors were not the killers, the jury took the unsupported word of the grieving mother and sentenced both, one to prison and the son to death. Though her husband denied at trial that it was the Jordanos that had attacked them, and Rosie Cortimiglia admitted under questioning that her memory was affected, the unsupported word of a mother who had lost her child swayed the jury. After all, everyone hoped it was the Jordanos so that this nightmare would end.

It seemed that Iorlando Jordano and his son Frank had been the first to respond to her screams and came to her rescue. Her thanks for their help was to accuse them of being the killers of her daughter. It later came out that she bore a business-related grudge against the two and in her state of mind after her injuries and the murder of her child, she was an easy one for the police to convince to testify against anyone, they did not seem to care who it might be, to bring this matter to a halt. In some quarters it Some thought if someone could be convicted, perhaps the real killer might go elsewhere. Eventually, after languishing jail and after Rosie Cortimiglia admitted in court that she had lied because she hated the Jordanos, both of the Jordanos were eventually absolved of the crimes, though both of their lives were ruined by the lies told in court.

THE SIXTH ATTACK

On August 10, 1919, Steve Boca, a New Orleans grocer was attacked, but survived. The first anyone knew about this attack was when Boca staggered form his home to the nearby room of Frank Genusa. Boca's skull was split open and he was bleeding heavily. Genusa immediately call for help and Boca was transferred to the Charity Hospital. Though he recovered from his wounds, he was unable to tell investigator anything about his attacker. He could only remember waking up to see a dark figure leaning over him and the axe coming at his head.

Even though the crime scene exhibited all the signs that it was an Axeman attack, the police demonstrated some frustration and a lack of due care regarding who they accused. The immediately arrested Frank Genusa for the attempted murder of Boca. When Boca vehemently defended his friend, he police were forced to dismiss the charges.

THE SEVENTH ATTACK

On the evening of September 2, a New Orleans druggist by the name of William Carlson was sitting up in his bed reading. He heard a sound at his back door and, gun in hand, answered the door, calling out for whoever was at the door to make himself known. When no one responded, he fired through the door aiming for where someone had to be standing in order to reach the backdoor.

Since the whole neighborhood was one edge as a result of the murders, the sound of the gunshot brought the police quickly and while no one was found in the backyard of Carlson's home, and no sign that Carlson had hit anyone with his wild shot, chisel marks were found on one of the panels of the back door. Many believe it was only his quick shot that saved him from being another victim of this dreaded killer.

Suddenly there was hope that perhaps Carlson had hit the mysterious Axeman. Perhaps, wounded, he had gone off by himself to die. Unfortunately, this was a false hope.

On September 3, 1919, 19-year-old Sarah Laumann was attacked but survived. She lived alone and would likely have bled to death from her wounds had not some neighbors, when she failed to answer her bell, broke into her home and found her unconscious in her bed, a bloody axe was found on the ground beneath an open window.

The young woman was rushed to the hospital and as a result of the quick treatment, she survived her injuries. It was determined by the doctors that she had a concussion from being hit in the head with the axe. Though she fully recovered she never regained her memory of the incident. Like all of the other victims that had survived the attacks by this mystery man, she could remember nothing about her attacker.

Though the killer had used an open window rather than chiseling a panel out of the door in this case, the police believed she was another victim of the dreaded Axeman. But with seven attacks to investigate, the authorities did not have a single clue as to the identity of the mysterious killer, the Jordano convictions notwithstanding.

THE EIGHTH ATTACK

Finally, on October 27, 1919, grocer Mike Pepitone was attacked and killed in his bed. Mrs. Pepitone claimed that she awoke to hear the sounds of a struggle coming from her husband's bedroom[6]. She said that she entered the adjoining room where her husband slept in time to see a man disappear through another door that led form her husband's bedroom. She screamed loudly which woke up their six young children who also began to scream.

Neighbors quickly summoned police. Who found a panel chiseled from the door and a bloody axe lying on the

---

[6] Apparently, Mr. and Mrs. Pepitone slept in separate bedrooms.

back porch. Mike Pepitone was dead. While his wife had seen the man running from the room, she was not able to give anything more than a general description.

There has been much speculation about the identity of the Axeman, but there has never been any proof as to his real identify. As was remarked earlier, it is interesting to note that even in the midst of a series of unsolved murders, one victim used this situation to try and get revenge on two completely innocent neighbors due to a dislike. Rather than thoroughly investigate the facts the police took her word for the identity of the killers (in this case) and both were sentenced to prison before it was discovered that she had lied. It was situations such as this that helped make this case so hard to solve.

It seemed that with the murder of Mike Pepitone, Jack the Axeman had ended his time in New Orleans. But there was an interesting postscript to this story.

UNFINISHED BUSINESS

On December 20, 1920, a former New Orleans resident by the name of Joseph Mumfre was strolling down a Los Angeles street. A heavily veiled woman dressed in black stepped out of a doorway and emptied a revolver into Mumfre. The killer then stood over Mumfre's dead body, making no attempt to escape.

When arrested, the woman first said that her name was Esther Albano and she would not say why she had murdered Mumfre. Then under questioning, she admitted that her name was Mrs. Mike Pepitone. She claimed that she had seen Joseph Mumfre run from her husband's room. She claimed that he was Jack the Axeman.

Later investigation shows that while Mumfre had spent much time in jail in New Orleans, he had quite a record, he had been out of jail on the date of each of the Axeman's murders. Police in New Orleans were jubilant, claiming that the Axeman was dead once and for all. However, many residents were not so sure. There was no proof that Mumfre had killed anyone and only Mrs. Mike Pepitone's word that he killed her husband.

Frankly, if there had been no evidence that Mumfre might not be the killer, then whether correct or not, as the police did, we could put closed on this case. However, in spite of rumors to the contrary, the killings did not stop, though the New Orleans police quit investigating. Consider the following, if you will -

ALEXANDRIA, LOUISIANA

Alexandria is a small town in Rapides Parish, Louisiana some two hundred miles northwest of New Orleans. It is located almost in the center of the state.

It was in December of the year 1920 when a very bloody murder took place in Alexandria. At about 1:00 AM on a cold December morning when Rosa Spero abruptly awoke, alarmed by a presence in her bedroom. She saw this figure attack her husband and then it turned its bloody weapon on her. She clearly saw the axe being swung at her and when it contacted with her head, she knew nothing else.

She awoke about 3 hours later to find her husband dead and her twenty-month-old daughter unconscious and bleeding. Her five boys were asleep and unharmed in the next room. Cradling her bleeding infant in her arms, Rosa ran from the house screaming for help. When the police were summoned, it was discovered that Joseph Spero had bled out.

The similarities between this attack and the New Orleans Axeman killings were startling, though it would seem not really appreciated by authorities. Joseph and Rosa Spero were the Italian proprietors of a grocery store as were most of the victims in New Orleans. The killer had come into the home through an open window, but he was carrying an axe taken form the backyard and a butcher knife taken from the grocery. He also left behind a railroad coupling pin showing at least a minimum connection with the railroad which ran through the town.

In the initial attack on Joseph Spero, the killer had broken his jaw and sliced his throat. Rosa Spero was cut as well but not as severely as her husband, her infant daughter died of her injuries. Like the New Orleans attacks, though there was cash in the house, nothing was taken. No suspects were identified, though a black carpenter who had done work for the Spero's was arrested when he was found to have blood on his clothing. After an investigation, he was released. No further suspects were identified.

DERIDDER, LOUISIANA

On January 14, 1921, in DeRidder, Louisiana, a small town about seventy miles southwest of Alexandria, Giovanni "John" Orlando was found sliced and bloody along with his wife and two small children. Giovanni was rush to the hospital, but he died in surgery.

Once again, the killer had entered the house through an open window, but though there was money available in the home, nothing was taken. He also left behind, alongside the body of Giovanni, his weapon of choice, a bloody axe.

Mary Orlando and her two children who had been sleeping in their parent's bed, were all badly cut, but survived their injuries. As in the earlier attacks, no suspects were identified, though the police immediately arrested a black man who was described as a half-witted Negro, however, he was soon released.

LAKE CHARLES, LOUISIANA

In the early hours of April 12, 1921, in Lake Charles, Louisiana, a small town some fifty miles south of DeRidder, another similar killing took place. It was around three o'clock in the morning when Marlena Scalisi ran screaming from her home calling for help. Her neighbors converged on her home to find Mrs. Scalisi literally covered with blood while her husband Frank was lying on the bed, his neck broken.

The Scalisi's had five children, one of whom slept with the parents while four slept in another room. The couple also ran a small grocery out of their home to supplement Frank's wages from his job at the Powell Lumber Company.

In this case, the murderer had entered the home through an open window carrying an old axe he had found in a neighbor yard. Upon entry, he used the axe to immediately kill Frank Scalisi and then raised his weapon to kill the sleeping mother and child. The problem for the killer was that the axe was old and had not been properly cared for by its owner. As his weapon descended toward the sleeping woman and child the head of the axe came off from the axe handle and hit the wall making a loud noise. The old wooden handle did hit the sleeping woman but did little harm.

At her scream, the intruder ran from the room. Marlena grabbed her sleeping baby and ran into the adjoining room where her ten-year-old daughter Mary was sleeping. She gave the baby to Mary before running outside to call for help from the neighbors.

Mary, who had been awakened by the noise and the screams got a good look at the assailant and described him as short, stout and Black. This of course raises questions about whether or not this was the Axeman of New Orleans, who had been described by more than one witness as being a white man.

There is no question that the modus operandi in the reported axe murders were similar enough to support the thesis that the same man did all of these killings, however, none of the victims could identify who attack them and the few witnesses were of little help. Though several were arrested and two were tried and convicted, it was later clear that the witnesses had lied in order to get the two convictions and were forced to later retract their testimony. Officials were just happy to be able to mark case closed on these murders and would have indicted a ham sandwich if it would have mollified the terrified public, evidence be damned. But whoever the killer known as Jack the Axeman might have been he was never identified and certainly his identity has never brought to light over the years.

CHAPTER THREE
THE BEAUTIFUL CIGAR GIRL

This next unsolved case was actually made famous by none other than Edgar Allen Poe in his work *The Mystery of Marie Roget*[7]. Though he did nothing to solve the case, he did call national attention to the matter.

Putting Poe's story aside for the moment, the actual murder victim was a beautiful young woman by the name of Mary Cecilia Rogers. She was believed to have been born in 1820 in Lyme, Connecticut and was found dead on July 28, 1841 when her lifeless body was pulled from the Hudson River. Though her murder was never solved, it became a national sensation involving a number of prominent people.

---

[7] Published in 1842

All who knew her agreed that Mary Rogers was a truly beautiful young woman. She worked in a tobacco store in New York City and was frankly showcased by the proprietor as an incentive to get more customers since it was clear that her beauty brought in a large number of customers, many very distinguished men of the time, who might not otherwise have favored this store with their trade if she had not been there to help them with their purchases.

Though there were no contemporary rumors of her having any affairs with some of her famous and wealthy customers, that was certainly a possibility. When her body was found dumped in the Hudson River, most assumed that she had been the victim of gang violence and the police did not attempt to dissuade those who reached this conclusion.

This would probably have been the end of the story had not a witness come forward to claim that Mary had been dumped in the river after dying during a failed abortion attempt. It was true that her boyfriend's suicide note suggested a possible involvement on his part, but there was never any evidence revealed that she might have been pregnant.

Mary lived in a boardinghouse run by her mother, Phoebe Rogers. Her father died in a steamboat explosion when she was 17 years old. Deciding that she needed to obtain employment, in part to help her mother, Mary obtained a job at a tobacco shop owned by John Anderson. She received a very generous salary, in large part due to her beauty, not for any skills she might possess in the way of retail experience.

It should also be noted that her customers were not shy in expressing their admiration for her beauty. One well to do individual spoke of spending an entire afternoon in the store exchanging teasing glances with the young woman, while another even published a poem in the New York Herald discussing her heaven-like smile. She found favor with the likes of James Fenimore Cooper, Washington

Irving, and Fitz-Greene Halleck, an American poet and the personal secretary and advisor to John Jacob Astor.

In addition to the involvement of such prominent men of the day, there were also a number of news reports that seemed to mark her as somewhat unstable[8]. For example, on October 5, 1838, the *New York Sun* reported that Miss Mary Cecilia Rogers had disappeared from her home[9]. According to the *Sun*, Phoebe Rogers, Mary's mother had reportedly found a suicide note which the local coroner analyzed and said revealed a deep and unalterable determination to destroy herself[10].

However, on October 6, 1838, the *Times and Commercial Intelligence* printed a story that said that the disappearance of Mary Rogers was a hoax and that she only went to visit a friend living in Brooklyn. Of course, there was

---

[8] It is also interesting that a mere clerk in a tobacco shop would rate such news coverage.
[9] Sova, Dawn B., Edgar Allen Poe: A to Z, Checkmark Books, New York 2001.
[10] Stashower, Daniel, The beautiful Cigar Girl, Penguin Books, New York, 2006

no evidence supporting either the disappearance or the friend living in Brooklyn.

It should also be noted that it was the *New York Sun* that was involved in the [Great Moon Hoax of 1835](#) which referred to a series of six articles beginning August 25, 1835, which reported the discovery of life and a civilization on the Moon. These discoveries, which was supposedly reprinted from the *Edinburgh Courant*, were attributed to the astronomer Sir John Herschel. Unfortunately for the Sun, these articles turned out to be false, they were said to have actually been written by Richard Adams Locke, a reporter who worked for the Sun.

Many believed the story of the disappearance of Mary Rogers was itself another hoax. When she returned to work, one paper reported that it was a major publicity stunt orchestrated by John Anderson.

On July 25, 1841, Mary Rogers told her fiancé, Daniel Payne that she was going to visit her aunt and some other family members[11]. However, on July 28, 1841, the police found Mary's corpse floating in the Hudson River near Hoboken, New Jersey. Due to the prominent people she associated with, it was no wonder that the case gained national attention.

The details of the case suggested that she had been murdered, or perhaps her body was dumped in the river by abortionist Madame Restell[12] after a failed procedure[13], though there was no evidence that she had been pregnant. It should also be remembered that in 1841, abortions were not illegal in New York, so why dump the body in the river? It would have been much easier just to call the police and say she died during the procedure. No harm no foul.

---

[11] Sova, Dawn B., Edgar Allen Poe: A to Z, Checkmark Books, New York 2001.

[12] The famed abortionist, Madame Restell was actually Ann Trow Lohman,
[13] Collins, Paul, The Murder of the Century, Random House, New York, 2011.

During the extended inquest held into Mary's death, Mary's fiancé, Daniel Payne, committed suicide on October 7, 1841, by overdosing on laudanum during a bout of heavy drinking. He allegedly left a suicide note that was found among the papers on his person where he died.

The wording of the note as reported in the press "*To the world – here I am on the very spot. May God forgive me for my misspent life*" was certainly peculiar. It led many to believe that he had something to do with Mary's death, though he had never been accused of involvement and no evidence ever surfaced that tied him to her death.

Certainly in 1841, if one was very careful, getting away with murder was a definite possibility. But in regard to the death of Mary Rogers, though it rose of national prominence, this story was something that was pushed out of the limelight as soon as possible. After all, some of her many admirers were men of national and perhaps international reputation. If she died during an abortion, who was the purported father; certainly, it could not have been any of these rich famous men?

As an example of those who could have been caught up in an above-board investigation, Fitz-Greene Halleck, a known admirer of the young woman was one of the initial trustees of the Astor Library, the mere smell of impropriety could have led to a major embarrassment not only for Halleck but for Astor himself. It should also be kept in mind that the law enforcement in New York at the time was not above taking a bribe to look the other way.

When Frederica Loss came forward in November of 1842 and claimed that Mary died during a failed abortion, the police not only refused to believe this would be witness, but also refused to even investigate the possibility.

Now this was a case tailor made for DNA if there ever was one. If Mary died during a botched abortion, though only the press claimed such a reason for her death, why did her mother or fiancé not come forward to support this possibility? Did her mother know if she was pregnant? The authorities never really investigated this possibility. It seemed that even local law enforcement that would become the famed NYPD wanted this case closed quickly. We may never know.

CHAPTER FOUR
THE VILLISCA AXE MURDERS

Between the years 1898 and 1912, entire families across the country were killed in their sleep with an axe. Due to the lack of communication between law enforcement agencies, each of these killing was actually treated as an isolated event. At the time the very concept of a serial killer was unheard of. However, without a doubt, the Villisca Axe Murders qualified as the work of a serial killer.

Out story begins with the Moore family, father Josiah, mother Sarah, and the children, Herman, Mary, Arthur and Paul, a well off and very well-known family in the town of Villisca, Iowa. In addition to everything else that the Moore had, they were also big workers in the local Presbyterian Church. In fact, on the evening of June 9^t, 1912, the entire family was at the Church for the Children' Day Program.

As was customary in this tight knit town, where everyone knew everyone, when the Moore family left for their home at around 9:30 PM, they took with them two friends of their ten-year-old daughter, Mary, eight-year-old Ina Stillinger, and twelve-year-old Lena Stillinger. Based on the distance the Moore house was from the church, the Moore family and their guests arrived home about 10:00 PM. The evidence showed that they had had a late snack of milk and cookies before going to bed.

It was early on the morning of June 10th when Mary Peckham, the Moore's elderly neighbor glanced out her window and became concerned. She immediately felt that something was not right, the Moore household was much too quiet, the curtains were drawn tightly over the windows and no one had come out to begin the morning chores. This was highly unusual.

Going outside, she saw that the chickens were still in their pens and she could hear the horses neighing in their stalls in the barn. As her concern rose, Mary walked slowly over to the front door and knocked loudly. She received no answer, so she tried the door to find that it was locked. She tried to peek in the windows, but the curtains were drawn down tightly. She was positive something was badly wrong.

Returning to her own home, Mary Peckham summoned Ross Moore, Josiah Moore's brother. He went to the front door and knocked loudly, even shouting for his brother, but he received no response either. His own concern now rising, he used his own key to open the front door and entered the darkened house, leaving Mary on the front porch.

Slowly and quietly, Ross crossed the front parlor and opened the door to the downstairs guest room. Inside he found two bodies lying in the bed, their faces covered with an overcoat. The headboard of the bed was covered with cast off blood. Not wanting to explore any further, Ross returned to the front porch and told Mary that something terrible had happened. He asked her to contact the local peace officer, Hank Horton.

It was some time before Horton arrived, but he was accompanied by the Presbyterian Minister, Wesley Ewing and Dr. J. Clark Cooper and Dr. Edgar Hough. The men conducted a search of the house and found that everyone inside was dead. The entire Moore family as well as the two Stillinger girls had been beaten to death with the blunt side of an axe to the point that their skulls has been obliterated.

Even the most sympathetic viewers would call the ensuing investigation something of a circus. However, in spite of the confusion, there were some useful clues found. Though nothing suggested a motive for these killings, it appeared that the entire family had been murdered in their sleep sometime between midnight and five in the morning. It appeared that the killer or killers had taken an oil lamp from a cupboard and bent the wick to keep the illumination dim enough to not wake the victims, but bright enough to see what he or she was doing.

Circumstances suggested that the killings had begun with Josiah and Sarah in the master bedroom and then moved to the bedroom next to their parents and killed the four Moore children. Last to be killed were the two Stillinger girls in the guestroom downstairs.

It appeared that the killer had been in the Moore's barn for some time, watching the house, waiting for the family to go to bed and fall asleep. Then he, or she, had taken Josiah Moore's own axe and entered the house through an unlocked back door.

Evidence suggested that 12-year-old Lena Stillinger may have been the only one of the victims to wake up during the attack. From her position on the bed, it appeared that she had tried to wiggle away from the attack. Her nightgown was pushed up around her waist and her undergarments were under the bed. There was no evidence that she had been raped, through it was impossible to rule out a sexual motive for the killings.

The partially cleaned but still bloody axe was found in the guest bedroom, along with part of a broken key chain. Inexplicably, a two-pound slab of bacon wrapped in a dish towel was found propped against one wall.

In the kitchen, a plate of uneaten food was found sitting beside a bowl of bloody water, which suggested that the killer had taken the time to prepare himself a meal, though, apparently, he did not eat it. It was assumed that he had washed his hands in the bowl of bloody water.

Inexplicably, the killer had covered the crushed heads of each victim with fabric. In the case of Josiah and Sarah, he used blankets with the children it was various pieces of clothing. The killer had also taken the time to cover all the mirrors and windows in the house with aprons and pieces of clothing that he had taken form various dressers around the house.

One final factor to be considered was that the investigation determined that the murder went back to each body after killing them to destroy each skull with numerous vicious blows of the axe. The raising of the axe had been so vicious that there were multiple gouges found in the ceiling above the Moore's beds

From the fact that nothing was missing, except for the keys to the house which had been used to lock all of the doors by the killer when the left, it was clear that theft had not been the reason for the murders. This left the police baffled in determining the reason for such a vicious attack. It seemed to them that the attack had been far too brutal to be random.

In looking for a motive, suspicion soon fell on Frank F. Jones, a prominent member of the community and a State Senator. Jones had once owned a farm equipment business and Josiah Moore had worked for him for seven years as an equipment salesman. However, Moore left Jones' employment and opened his own business, taking Jones' most profitable account. There were also unsubstantiated rumors that Moore had also enjoyed the charms of Frank's daughter-in-law. The end result was that the two men hated each other to the point that they would cross the street not to have to come in contact with each other.

The other reason that Jones was a prime suspect was that he was Methodist. Therefore, the Presbyterians were all sure that Frank was the killer, while all of the Methodists were just as positive that he was innocent. Feelings ran so high that Detective James Wilkerson of Kansas City who had been asked to look into the matter suggested that a grand jury be convened to determine once and for all if Senator Frank had any involvement with the murders.

From written records, it was clear that Wilkerson did not really believe that Frank had committed the murders, but he believed that it was very possible that Frank had hired someone to commit these heinous crimes. He also though he knew who Frank had hired, a man by the name of William "Blackie" Mansfield. Mansfield had long been suspected of the axe murders of his own family in Blue Island, Illinois.

Unfortunately for Wilkerson's theory, payroll records revealed that Mansfield had been fourteen hundred miles away from Villisca on the day of the killings. Of course, even though Mansfield was cleared, it did not stop many from believing that Frank had paid someone else to kill the Moores. In the end though the Grand Jury did not return a true bill indicting Frank, the investigation and the rumors essentially ruined his political career.

OTHER SUSPECTES

Under pressure to solve this heinous crime, authorities grasped at any possible clue that might reveal the killer. There was another suspect in the town who many suspected might be involved. Though he had no personal beef with the Moores, his actions were odd enough to gain the attention of all who saw him and as evidence piled up, he seemed tailor made to fit the bill for the killer.

This particular person was a wandering English preacher by the name of Lyn George Jacklin Kelly who was known to authorities as a sexual deviant. In fact, he had been in and out of mental institutions his entire life. Two days before the Moores were killed, Kelly had been caught peeping into windows around town and there were witnesses who swore that Kelly had been at the Presbyterian Church during the church function that the Moores had attended.

From the position and angles of the blows, investigators believed that the killer was left handed. Kelly was left handed. There was evidence that Kelly had caught a train out of Villisca around five o'clock in the morning before the bodies had been discovered. Witnesses also claimed that at about 5:19 AM Kelly told a couple at the train station that a grisly murder had taken place in Villisca. This was about two hours before the bodies had been discovered.

It was also discovered that in a town down the train line Kelly had taken some bloodstained clothes to be dry cleaned.

Of course, there is a great deal of evidence that Kelly was not exactly playing with a full deck. A week after the murders he returned to Villisca, told authorities he was Scotland Yard and asked for a tour of the murder house. There is no record of the response of the local investigating officers.

Kelly was actually arrested for the murders in 1917 and after being interrogated, he signed a confession. Though this was though to end the matter, Kelly recanted his confession and the witnesses who claimed that Kelly had told them about the murders two hours before the bodies were discovered reversed their testimony.

A Grand Jury was convened which ended in a hung jury. A second Grand Jury eventually found that there was no evidence that directly tied Kelly to the murders. Eventually he was released.

Then there was a transient railway worker by the name of Andy Sawyer. He seemed obsessed with the killings to the point that his employer reported his erratic behavior to the police. He was a very strong candidate until it was found that he had been arrested for vagrancy in another town on the day of the murder.

Police even considered Josiah's brothers-in-law Sam Moyer and Roy Van Gilder. While this was a long shot, there was a rumor that Sam Moyer and Josiah were enemies, but it was determined that this was based entirely on hearsay. Additionally, Sam could prove that he had been in Nebraska on the day of the killings.

Finally, there was the possibility that the killing of the Moore family was part of a string of random slayings that had taken place across the Midwest in 1911 and 1912. During these years, there had been a strong of unsolved axe murders in various towns all located in close proximity to the railroads. It was also revealed that in these other killings there were a number of similarities to the Moore murders.

- Almost all of them were carried out with an axe or other weapons found outside the home of the victims and as in the Moore case, the weapon was left behind.
- The victims were all bludgeoned to death in their sleep.
- And a few of them had been sexually assaulted. In one case the nightgown was pushed up and the undergarments thrown under the bed just as in the case of Lina Stillinger.
- Most of the murders took place on a weekend, usually on Sunday as in the Moore murders[14].
- In some of the cases, the killer attempted or actually carried out a second attack in the same location. It should be noted that the woman who worked the

---

[14] It should be noted that the killings had a lot in common with the story of Jack the Axeman as well.

night shift at the Villisca telephone exchange reported that someone tried to gain entry at about 2:00 AM but then left.

- In five of the cases the killer had lain in wait for the victims and had lingered sometime after the killings.
- In four of the cases, the killer covered the victims' faces with blankets or clothing and had covered the mirrors or the windows.
- In three of the cases, the killer tried to wash the blood form his hands at the scene.
- In two of the cases, land with bent wicks were found in the homes just as at Villisca.

Logically speaking, due to the similarities, there is a strong case that the killings were done by the same person. But in the case of serial killer it is very hard to find the connections needed to make an arrest. Unfortunately, the Villisca Axe Murderer was never found. Another case where the gut of the investigating officials was not successful.

CHAPTER FIVE
THE MURDER OF MARY PHAGAN

The murder of 13-year-old Mary Phagan has always been a case involving wrongdoing on the part of court officials as well as corrupt and incompetent police work at every level. Though Leo Frank was convicted of her murder and then broken out of prison to be hung by a lynch mob, there is a great deal of evidence to indicate that Frank was framed by the police simply because he was Jewish, and the killer or killers got away.

By all accounts, Mary Phagan was a lovely young girl, who would have grown into a beautiful young woman. She was born June 1, 1899 into what was referred to as an established Georgia family of tenant farmers. As her father died prior to her birth, she was raised primarily by her mother, Frances Phagan. For her part, Frances moved her daughter several times in an attempt to establish a stable home life. In 1899, shortly after the birth of her daughter, she moved back to her hometown of Marietta, Georgia and then sometime in 1907, she moved to Eastpoint, Georgia where she opened a boarding house.

It must be remembered that the early 20th century was a time of child labor. Many jobs that today we would never dream of allowing a child to perform were in fact routinely filled with children during this time period as their wages were much less than those of an adult. So, it was that, at the tender age of 10 years old, Mary's mother allowed her to leave school to take a part time job at a textile factory. While the wages could not have been much, every penny was needed to help keep a roof over the family's head.

In 1912 things appeared to be getting better for the Phagans as Frances Phagan married John William Coleman, who moved his ready-made family to Atlanta.

In the Spring of 1912, Mary got what, to her, seemed a dream job with the National Pencil Company. She earned ten cents an hour operating a knurling machine which inserted rubber erasers into the metal tips of pencils. She was initially scheduled to work 55 hours per week[15]. While she would earn 5.50 cents per week if she worked a full shift (55 hours per week), in 1912, that was considered a decent wage for a child[16].

Her job location was on the second floor of the factory in a metal room which was located in a section called the tipping department. It was also located directly across the hall from the office of the Superintendent of the Pencil factory, Leo Frank.

---

[15] At the time of her murder, Georgia was the only state that permitted children as young as ten to work eleven hours a day in the factories. An attempt to raise the minimum age to 14 was defeated in the state legislature.

[16] In 1912, the average wage was 22 cents per hour for an adult make worker. Children and women were paid about the same as women in 1912 earned only 50-60% of the wages a male would earn in the same job.

On April 21, 1913, Mary was laid off due a shortage of brass sheet metal. Without this sheet metal, should not run her machine or install the erasers on the tip of the pencil. Since there was little in the way of job security for unskilled laborers in 1913, she was left wondering how to earn a living. Since every penny was important to this young wage earner, she was not prepared to forego anything she may have earned at the Pencil Company. So, it was that on the afternoon of April 26, 1913, Mary Phagan made a fateful trip to the company to claim her last paycheck, which amounted to a grand total of $1.20[17]. This was also the same day that she met her killer.

As near as can be determined, the murder took place either late in the evening of Saturday, April 26, 1913 or very early on Sunday Morning, April 27th. The body was discovered by Newt Lee, the Night Watchman, at about 3:00

---

[17] Author unknown, The Frank Case, Published by the Atlanta Publishing Company, Atlanta, GA. 1913.

AM on April 27th. At that hour, of course, the factory was deserted, dark and cold. Though it was late April, in Atlanta, Georgia, it could still get quite cold at night as it was this night since the heat in the factory, which came from a boiler in the basement, was set low to conserve heating fuel and thus lower operating costs.

There are actually two different stories about how and why Newt Lee found the body of Mary Phagan. The first story was that he was the Night Watchman and it was Lee's duty to make rounds of each area of each floor of the deserted plant each hour. He had to punch a time clock every thirty minutes on each floor, the only light, a hand carried lantern.

The second story about how and why he found the body was that Lee had to go to the toilet and the only place he could go was located in the basement. However, based on the earliest account of this case, this was patently not true as there were bathrooms in the work areas for the employees.

According to reports, Lee was tired this night, even though he had been given some unexpected time off in the afternoon by Leo Franks. Having been on the job for some months, he had become used to wandering around the huge factory building in the dark, his footsteps and his own breathing the only sounds he heard. So, he could not have been said to be especially alert as he patrolled the dark, deserted second floor, punched the time clock and started down the narrow stairs toward the first floor.

Finding nothing out of the ordinary on the dark deserted first floor, Lee opened the trap door over the scuttle hole that led to the pitch-black basement. Taking a firm grip on the metal handle of the gently swinging lantern, he slowly descended the narrow ladder to the basement of the silent factory. If there was an area where he was especially cautious, it was this very dark, silent tomb-like area. The basement was lit after a fashion, as there was a gas jet that was to always be left burning, though tonight it was turned down low.

Slowly, he turned, his lantern light illuminating each corner of the very dark area. The first three corners were empty as always, but when he turned his lantern toward the boiler, he saw something that should not have been there. Thinking he eyes were playing tricks on him, he moved closer to the boiler to better examine what lay there and then froze[18]. He was looking at the body of a child.

The body Newt Lee discovered was that of Mary Phagan. According to the police reports, the girl was discovered in the rear of the basement near an incincrator. Her dress was pulled up around her waist and a strip of her petticoat had been torn off and wrapped around her neck. Her little face was blackened and scratched, her head was bruised and battered as if she had been severely beaten.

---

[18] Ibid

A 7-foot trip of 1/4 inch wrapping cord was tied into a loop around her neck and was buried ¼ inches deep showing that she had apparently died from strangulation. Her underwear was still around her slim hips, but it was stained with blood and torn open. Her skin was covered with ashes and direct from the floor of the basement. The initial impression of the investigating officers is that she and her killer had struggled in the basement before she was overpowered.

There was a service ramp that at the rear of the basement that led to a sliding door which opened into the alley behind the building. During the investigation it was discovered that the lock of this sliding door had been tempered with so that it could be opened from the outside without being unlocked. Even though there was much discussion that only someone with access to the plant could have entered the basement, this was clearly not true.

During the investigation, it was also discovered that there were bloody fingerprints on the door and prints were also found on a metal pipe that had been used as a crowbar.

Officers Rogers and W.T. Anderson, along with a reporter who had been sleeping in the back seat of Roger's car as well as Officers Dobbs and Brown who were picked up along the way, arrived at the silent Pencil Factory, still dark in these early morning hours. After a period of pounding on the front door, they were admitted by a very shaken Newt Lee, whose eyes reflected his shock at finding a dead body.

The officers demanded to be taken to the dead body and so it was that, guns drawn, the four officers followed the terrified Night Watchman across the main floor of the silent factory to the ladder that led to the equally silent basement. Lee led them down the leader to the basement and pointed with a shaky hand toward the boiler area.

"That's the body," he croaked.

The four officers bent over the small body. She was lying face down across a pile of saw dust, her head was pointed toward the front, her feet lying diagonally cross the pile toward the right rear corner of the basement. Her face, black with grime was turned toward the wall.

Gently, the big officers knelt down and gently turned the tiny body and only then saw the extent of her injuries. According to their description, her hair was in shreds, but it was the unmistakable hair of a white person. Her hair was matted and stained dark with blood that had flowed from a blow on the back of her head[19].

The deceased had been wearing a blue-ribbon in her hair which was now wilted, dirty and blood stained. She was wearing a silk lavender dress which was now smeared with blood and grimy from its contact with the floor of the

---

[19] Author unknown, The Frank Case, Published by the Atlanta Publishing Company, Atlanta, GA. 1913.

basement. One small white slipper was still dangling from her right foot.

As her head fell back, the officers could now see the heavy cord wrapped tightly around her slender neck, a makeshift gag torn from her own dress wrapped her head and filled her mouth. Her underskirt was ripped to shreds, the supporter for one of her white stockings was broken while the stocking itself bagged down almost to the knee of the slim leg.

As Sergeant Brown examined the body as well as he could in the dim light of the lantern, Sergeant Dobbs made what was described as a thorough search of the cellar floor his eyes probing the darkness in the very dim light available to him. A few feet from the body, he found the other shoe lying forlorn on the dirty floor. Near an elevator shaft he found the hat the had left home wearing. Then he made what was described as a big discovery.

Lying discarded on the dirt floor were two dirty pieces of paper which Sergeant Dodd quickly grabbed with his bare hands. He also never marked the exact location where he found each scrap of paper.

On these scraps someone had very crudely scrawled messages.

The first message said: "*He said he wood love me laid down like the night witch did it. But that long tall black negro did it by hisself.*"

The second message read: "*Mamtma that negro hired down here did this I went to get water and he pushed me down this hole a long tall negro black that has it woke longr lean tall negro I write while play with me.*"

The two messages certainly made no sense to the officers. Had the killer written these two messages? Did the victim? Certainly, the eyes of each officer present turned to stare at the Night Watchman. It was W.T. Anderson who broke the ensuing silence.

"Nigger, you done this," he accused the Night Watchman in a rough voice, grabbing the man by the shoulder.

Newt Lee was stunned. He shook his head wildly and croaked out a response.

"Fore God, Ah didn't, white folks!" he was said to have responded.

Ignoring the denial, it was only seconds later that Anderson slapped the cuffs on Lee with a resounding click. Newt Lee was arrested for the murder of the currently unknown female victim. Case closed – well maybe!

By 5:00 AM, the body of the unknown white female had been transferred to the morgue and Newt Lee was safely behind bars. Another case closed through the brilliant detective work of Atlanta's finest. Of course, they still had to identify the victim, and prove that Lee was guilty of her murder, but in 1913 Georgia, color and religion counted more toward proving guilt that such a silly thing as evidence. Newt Lee was Black, so in the minds of the four officers the case was closed, well, almost.

Officer Rogers stated to the other officers at the crime scene that he knew someone who worked at the Pencil factory who might be able to identify the dead girl. He was referring to his sister-in-law Grace Hix. Rogers went and got her and took her to the morgue. Grace Hix took one look at the dead girl and blurted out *"It's the little girl that worked at the machine next to me – It's Mary Phagan."* Then Grace Hix fainted.

While the identification was taking place, other officers had been at the crime scene. At about 5:30, Detective Starnes called up Leo Frank, the superintendent, at his home and told him that something had happened at the factor. Detective Starnes said they would send a car to get him.

According to what was said by Rogers and Detective John Black, when they arrived at the Frank home, Mrs. Frank opened the door and then almost immediately Leo Frank joined them. He was almost dressed except for his collar and his tie. He also appeared, at least to them, to be extremely nervous, constantly rubbing his hands[20] which they found suspicious.

The three men got into Rogers' car and left the Frank home. Rogers asked Frank if he knew a girl named Mary Phagan and he responded that he would look at the factory payroll and see if that name was listed as an employee.

Arriving at the Pencil Factory, Leo Frank went directly to his office, pulled out an employee ledger and confirmed that Mary Phagan was, or had been employed there. At this point, he seemed to remember Mary and said that she had come in to get her pay. The stenographer left at

---

[20] In hindsight, the Detectives considered this nervousness highly suspicious.

noon and the office boy had left a few minutes later and he thought that Mary had come in about 12:15. He also mentioned that someone who had been fired, J. M. Gantt had also come in Saturday morning to pick up a pair of shoes he had left behind and that he thought that Mary knew him. Police immediately began looking for J.M. Gantt.

Certainly, throughout his time with the police, Leo Franks acted nervous and nervously talked. This was later viewed as a sign of guilt or at least a guilty conscious. In fact, N. V. Darley, the general foreman of the plant who Franks had called to come in, said that Franks was actually trembling.

The story of Mary's last day was pieced together from various witnesses. It was Memorial Day, a holiday, so it was the first holiday that Mary had been able to enjoy, though now that she was laid off, everyday would be a holiday until she found another job.

Mary had planned to go get her pay from the factory and then spend the rest of the day watching the Confederate Veterans parade down Peachtree Street. According to her mother, Mary had a lunch of cabbages and biscuit before leaving for the factory. She was said to have boarded a street car about noon.

At this point it should be commented that Mary's attire was certainly rather dressy for someone who was going to a factory and watch a parade. It was perhaps what those in the south used to call Sunday go to meeting attire. A Lavender dress, white hose, a bow in her hair, this was not casual dress by any means. Was she planning on meeting a paramour? Certainly, this was never addressed by the police.

Once on the street car, Mary met a neighbor boy, George Epps. They sat together on the car and before she left the car, she promised to meet her friend at 1:00 PM and go watch the parade with him.

At Marietta and Forsyth Streets, Mary left the street car. She was about a block from the factory building at this point. That was the last that anyone saw of Mary Phagan.

Late that evening, George Epps went to Mary's house to find out why she hadn't met him at the parade. He found that her mother was very worried because Mary had not come home. J.W. Coleman, her step-father went into town to check all of the places that Mary might have gone but to no avail. No one had seen the young girl.

It was not until early Sunday morning, April 27th that Helen Ferguson, a neighbor came to tell Frances Phagan that Mary was dead. Mr. Coleman immediately rush down to the Bloomfield Mortuary where he viewed the body, confirming that Mary Phagan was dead.

When word spread of Mary's murder, the largest crowds in Atlanta's history, to that time, came to view the body, over 20,000. Hundreds more came to view the body at the funeral in Marietta.

Prior to the funeral, physicians made an examination of parts of Mary's body, though their results were kept secret until the trial. Onn Tuesday, April 29th, Mary Phagan was laid to rest in the old family cemetery in Marietta. However, in a shocking turn of events, on May 7th, the body was exhumed at the order of the state solicitor and detailed examination was made of the stomach and other vital organs by H.F. Harris, a physician from the state board of health. Again, the findings from this unusual examination were kept secret until the trial, which took place almost three months later.

THE INVESTIGATION

Though police were sure that they had got their man with arrest of Newt Lee, they were forced to examine some of the hundreds of tips that flooded their headquarters. In addition to the so-called murder notes, Lee had been able to tell officers that it was a white girl when he had said he had not examined the body and according to the officers Mary was so grimy that it was impossible to tell what color she was from any distance. Lee claimed he knew she was white based on her hair. It should also be mentioned that in their initial investigation of the crime scene that much of evidence from there had been compromised by the first officers on the scene.

In the darkness of the basement, police had trampled a trail in the dirt that led form the elevator shaft along which police believed the killer had dragged the body. Footprints that were found around the body were never identified and the bloody fingerprints on the sliding door were never properly investigated. The author, or authors, of what the press was calling the murder notes, were never ascertained.

There were also questions that arose on how police found blood spots on the second floor of the factory around the machine upon Mary Phagan worked. However, even if this was true, what would be the relevance of this blood when she had been laid off and was no longer operating that machine. What would have been her reason to be around the machine at this point, especially dressed in what were probably her best clothes?

Then it was stated that blood spots had been found on the first floor near the elevator shaft. This supported a theory that she had been murdered and then taken to the basement where her body was dumped.

A witness came forward who said that he had seen Mary Phagan at 12:10 PM walking along Forsyth Street with a former street car conduct named Arthur Mullinax. E.L. Sentell, an employee of the C.J. Kemper Grocery, told police he knew Mary, had known her for years and that there was no doubt that it was she he had seen with Mullinax. Mullinax was arrested and thrown in jail on suspicion of murder.

Then police arrested J. M. Gantt on suspicion. He had worked at the factory, knew Mary and did not have a solid alibi. His sister, Mrs. C.F. Terrell said that he had stayed at her house Friday night, but then she gave conflicting statements about his movements after that. So now there were three people arrested in regard to Mary's Murder.

On Monday, April 28th, the Pencil factory hired the local Pinkerton Detectives to help the police solve the crime. That same morning, the Coroner, Paul Donehoo convened the Coroner's jury in the metal room of the pencil factory for a viewing of the possible murder scene. The jury was adjourned immediately after they saw the room.

On May 1, at the Coroner's inquest, Mullinax's fiancé, Pearl Robinson came forward and stated that it was she that had been walking with Mullinax on Forsyth Street at 12:10 PM on that particular day. Face with this E.L. Sentell retracted his statement. Mullinax was freed. Gantt was freed as well when it turned out the evidence against him was not solid.

On Tuesday, April 29th, Leo Frank, the superintendent of the National Pencil factory was arrested on suspicion of the murder of Mary Phagan. Little did he know when the cell door clamed shut behind him that he would never see freedom again. In the Georgia legal system, accusation equaled guilt, the trial was a formality. Which is unfortunately somewhat true today.

The evidence against him could not be said to be conclusive. Certainly, it would not be sufficient for an arrest in any other jurisdiction in this country, but this was Georgia, a place where race and position mattered a great deal. The police felt they had built a solid case against the man.

- By his own admission, Frank was the last man known to have seen Mary Phagan alive.
- He appeared nervous when Newt Lee came to the factory early in the afternoon.
- He called Newt Lee over the telephone during the evening, something he had never done before.
- He was nervous when Gant came to the factory on Saturday afternoon,

- He was nervous when officers took him to the factory Sunday Morning.

Frankly, in a modern court, any fist year legal aid attorney could have destroyed this case. But this was Georgia and behind the scenes, it was clear that it would make a lot of people happy if Franks was convicted, after all he was Jewish! If they could not pin the case on Newt Lee, a Black man, then who better than Frank.

Even though they had arrested Leo Frank, Atlanta police did not want to give up on their chief suspect, Newt Lee. In an effort to find additional evidence, police conducted a detailed search of Lee's home. In a burn barrel in back of his cabin, investigators discovered a shirt with dark stains on it. Investigators immediate declared it to be blood and Mary Phagan's blood at that. The blood was smeared high up on the armpits and the shirt appeared to have never been worn.

While police were initially jubilant over the discovery, they began to believe that the shirt may have been planted to incriminate Lee. The main problem with this evidence was that police could not explain was why the shirt appeared not to have been worn after the blood was smeared on it. For his part, Newt Lee denied ever having seen the shirt before claiming that the one he had on he had worn for a week. Police finally decided that Franks had arrange the shirt to be planted to incriminate Lee.

It appears that there was no single piece of evidence that pointed the blame to Frank, but there was a lot of small things. According to Steve Oney[21] in his book *And The Dead Shall Rise: The Murder of Mary Phagan and the Lynching of Leo Frank* the evidence against Leo Frank consisted of the following:

---

[21] Oney, Steve, *And The Dead Shall Rise: The Murder of Mary Phagan and the Lynching of Leo Frank,* Patheon Books, 2003.

- The charges were dropped against Mullinax and Gantt;
- The rumors that Mary Phagan had been seen later than 12:15 on the street were discounted which made Frank the last person to admit to seeing Mary alive;
- Frank called in the Pinkertons;
- A shifting view of Newt Lee's role in the matter.

The police were willing to shift things around the make their case. Now it was believed that Newt Lee was actually Frank's accomplice in the murder. Authorities arranged a face to face meeting between Newt Lee and Leo Frank in the hopes that one or the other would make an incriminating statement. Nothing conclusive came from this meeting, but the police viewed it as further factor implicating Frank as the murderer.

During the Coroner's Inquest, the newspaper boy George Epps said that Mary had mentioned to him that Frank had once winked at her and looked suspicious. There was no evidence submitted supporting these events and no explanation of what Mary allegedly meant when she called him suspicious. As a matter of law, this statement by Epps was hearsay at its finest and certainly under the Rules of Evidence it was not admissible at trial, but in a Georgia courtroom hearsay is how many cases are decided.

To make matter worse for Frank, several of the women who worked at the pencil factory said that Frank had flirted with them and one claimed that she had been propositioned. Of course, none of these witnesses had anything to back up their claims, not even being able to furnish dates of when these evets are supposed to have taken place. The detectives even had to admit that they had so far obtained no conclusive evidence or even any clues in the baffling mystery. Based on this nothing of a case, the Coroner ordered that Lee and Frank were to be detained[22].

---

[22] Dinnerstein, Leonard, The Leo Frank Case, University of Georgia Press, 1987.

In May, William J. Burns, of the Burns Detective Agency traveled to Atlanta to offer assistance in solving the case. However, that same month his firm withdrew from the case due to the petty politics that continually interfered with the investigation. The agency quickly became uncomfortable with the many societal implications in the case, one of the most important being that since Frank was a rich Jew so that meant he could buy off the police and bring in private detectives to get him off.

There was also said to be intense animosity between the police and the private detectives hired by the Pencil factory that even resulted in the police following the private detectives to insure they did not plant evidence that would clear Frank.

The police left no stone unturned in their efforts to build a case against Frank. They even had Frank strip and allow his body to be examined for wounds of any sort. The police found none, nor did they find any blood on the suit that Frank wore that day and none on any clothing at his home.

In spite of this, it seems that Officers were positive Frank was the culprit and left no stone unturned to make their case. Officers questioned Jim Conley, the factory's janitor and even though he admitted he lied on several occasions, based on what he had to say after some coaching, used his statements to build the case against Leo Frank. There were also indications that the third degree[23] had been used on several witnesses in order to get them to make the statements the police desired. As we shall see shortly, the third degree was used on several potential witnesses to build the case against Leo Frank.

THE EVIDENCE

One important facet of the prosecution's case was the timeline they had worked so hard to establish. However,

---

[23] The term third degree is a euphemism for torture, in other words, inflicting pain, physical or mental, to extract confessions of statements. In 1931, the Wickersham Commission found that the use of the third degree was widespread in the United States.

even the most basic overview showed several problems with the timeline.

Based upon the stomach contents, the prosecution argued that Mary Phagan had died between 12:00 and 12:15 PM. One off the prosecution's main witnesses, Monteen Stover, testified that she had gone to Frank's office to get her paycheck. She was positive she waited there from 12:05 PM to 12:10 PM and did not see Frank in his office. According to the prosecution, Frank was busy killing Mary Phagan at this time which was why he was not in his office[24].

The testimony of George Epps was used to establish what time Mary was said to have gotten off the trolley. He was adamant that she had left the trolley at 12:07 PM exactly. However, both the motorman, W.M. Matthews and the conductor W. T. Hollis testified that Phagan got off the

---

[24] Of course, Monteen Stover was not asked to prove she had been in Frank's office or show anything to corroborate how long she was in the office or even if she was in the office.

trolley at 12:10. They both also testified that George Epps[25] had not been on the trolley that day. However, the Prosecution refused to question Epp's testimony as they needed it for their timeline.

According to testimony offered at trial, it takes 3-4 minutes from the trolley stop to walk to the factory. If the Motorman and the conductor were correct regarding the time that Mary left the trolley, the earliest she could have arrived at the factory, unless she ran from the trolley stop to the factory which was never inquired into, was approximately 12:15 PM. By this time, Monteen Stover, by her own testimony had left Frank's office which makes her testimony irrelevant. It also shows that for the time of death to be accurate, Mary had to be killed the moment she stepped into the factory, which does not fit with the prosecution's theory.

---

[25] Wrist watches were a rarity in 1913, especially among the young. No one inquired how Georgia Epps was so sure it was exactly 12:07.

However, since the authorities were adamant that he killed Mary, adjustments to stories and statements were made. Part of the problem was that the members of the Coroner's jury, the Grand Jury and the Trial Jury had been bombarded by press reports and police statements that Frank was guilty, his chances of a fair trial were almost nil.

The trial was almost a formality since testimony that should have cleared Frank was ignored time and time again. Lemmie Quinn, the foreman of the metal room, also testified that he spoke to Frank in his office at 12:20 PM. Frank had not mentioned Quinn's visit when he was first interviewed by police on April 27th. At the coroner's inquest, Frank testified that Quinn had arrived less than 10 minutes after Phagan left his office. At trial, Frank testified that it was less than 5 minutes after Phagan left his office that Quinn arrived.

Defense witnesses testified that it would have taken at least thirty minutes to murder Phagan, take the body to the basement, return to the office, and write the so-called murder notes, but Frank's time was fully accounted for between 11:30 AM and 1:30 PM. The crucial time was between 12:00 PM and 12:15 PM and if he met with Quinn at 12:20 PM, and Quinn said that Frank was sitting at his desk working when he arrived, Frank was certainly not writing murder notes and showed no signs of having just committed a murder. If these witnesses were telling the truth, Leo Frank could not possibly have killed Mary Phagan.

The prosecution dealt with this problem with their timeline and witnesses that tended to clear Frank by simply ignoring them. In the case of Quinn, the Prosecutor accused Quinn of lying, naturally without submitting any proof supporting this charge and then reminded the jury that Frank had not mentioned Quinn in his statements to the police, so according to the Prosecution, this proved that Quinn's testimony had to be fraudulent.

Race certainly played a part in this trial and the prosecution did nothing to stop it. The prosecution focused a portion of their case on what they called Frank's sexual behavior, which was based entirely on the unsupported testimony of Jim Conley, the plant janitor.

Much was also made in the press about the sexual desires of Jews for white, gentile, women[26]. According to Lindemann in his work, there was a developing stereotype of wanton, young Jewish males who hungered for fair-haired Gentile women. While this was said to a familiar stereotype in Europe, this unreasoned fear of Jewish sexuality threatening white Gentile females reached Atlanta in the 1890s with the arrival of a wave of eastern European Jews[27].

This alleged Jewish desire for white Gentile women, tacitly supported by the prosecution's case, inflamed those who had decided that Frank had to guilty and directly led to the truly disgraceful actions that happened later.

---

[26] Lindemann, Albert S., The Jew Accused: The Anti-Semitic Affairs (Dreyfus, Bellis, Frank) Cambridge University Press, 1991
[27] It also might be noted that this stereotype was very similar to the belief that freed Blacks lusted after the flower of southern beauty.

As for the racial prejudice part, actually both legal teams, defense as well as prosecution made use of racial stereotypes during the trial. The defense, who believed that Conley was either the killer or helped kill Mary, pictured Conley as a new kind of African American, anarchic, degraded and dangerous. The Prosecutor, on the other hand, pictured Conley as a familiar type of old Negro, like a minstrel player or a plantation worker. It was maintained that being a Negro, Conley was not intelligent enough to concoct a complicated story, so what he said had to be the truth.

JIM CONLEY'S STORY

As mentioned earlier, the Prosecution based the bulk of its case on the testimony of Jim Conley, the factory janitor[28]. Evidence was found after the trial showing that it was probably Conley that killed Mary Phagan, however,

---

[28] According to Lindemann, the best evidence now available indicates that the real murderer was probably Jim Conley. It was theorized that after she left Frank's office, she met Conley who testimony showed was in the building who tried to get the girl to give him her pay envelope. When she refused, it was believed he killed her and took the money.

having been publicly committed to the guilt of Frank, and under tremendous pressure by the demands of the public that the "Jewish pervert" be hung, the evidence implicating Conley was ignored by the police[29].

Conley was first investigated and arrested when a witness, E. L. Holloway, the plant time keeper, reported that Conley had been seen washing red stains from a blue work shirt. Conley claimed that it was rust stains he was washing out of his shirt since he had been called to testify at the Coroner's Inquest and did not want to go in front of the Coroner's Jury a with a dirty shirt. Police saw no reason not to believe him, but he was locked up anyway.

In his initial statement to police, Conley maintained that he had not been anywhere near the factory on the day of the murder. He also told Detective Scott that he could not write a word when Scott asked him to write a few sentences

---

[29] Woodward, Corner Van, *Tom Watson: Agrarian Rebel*, Oxford University Press, 1963.

for comparison with the murder notes. Scott believed him when Conley said he could not write a word so police just let him sit in jail.

It was only after investigators began to get negative reports about Conley from other workers that they turned their attention to him again. It seemed that he had a long criminal record and was not liked at the factory. He also had a reputation for borrowing money and not paying it back. Of course, even this was not enough to get investigators to consider him a suspect until Scott found out from a clerk at the factory that Conley could both read and write.

Now that police knew that his original statement was not true, they gave him their full attention and even went so far as to give him the third degree. Finally, on Friday, May 23rd, Conley admitted that he knew how to write and gave officers a sample. A quick comparison made it clear that Conley had very likely written the murder notes that police had found at the crime scene. However, it was until the next morning that Conley changed his story.

It was 10:00 AM that Saturday morning when Conley sent for Detective Black. When Black arrived at Conley's cell, Conley said he had lied in his first statement to the police but that now he was going to tell the whole story. He said that he had written the so-called murder notes, but it was because Leo Frank had ordered him to do so. Conley said that Franks had promised that if he wrote the notes, Frank would send them to his mother and she would give Conley a job.

Conley was elated, he knew that Conley had just put the rope around Frank's neck and he, Black, would get the credit. The first thing he did was test Conley on his spelling and discovered that Conley's spelling of the various words in the murder notes was consistent with the original notes. There was no doubt that Conley had written the two murder notes. The main problem from the point of view of the police was that Conley swore that Frank asked him to write the notes on Friday, which suggested premeditation. It also suggested that Frank, Conley's boss at the factory, had confessed to Conley about killing the girl, which police did not believe.

Though the police knew that Conley was still lying, if he would allow them to coach him, the statement would seal the case against Frank. His second affidavit to the police helped solidify the case against Frank by at least confirming beyond a shadow of a doubt who had written the murder notes. However, there were still some gaps in Conley's story.

Deciding to get the full story out of Conley, the police subjected him to the third degree, though the defense claimed that the police actually took Conley to school to tell him what to say in his third affidavit. Certainly, his third attempt at making a formal statement, in spite of some remaining issues, firmly put the noose around Frank's neck.

In his third statement, Conley admitted that he had lied about meeting Frank on Friday (the premeditation angle was just simply to unbelievable) and said he met Frank on the street on Saturday. He said Frank had told him to follow him to the plant and hide in a wardrobe so that two women who were going to visit Frank would not see him. He further claimed that Frank dictated the notes for him to write. He went on to claim that after he wrote the notes, he left the plant and went to a movie. Police were concerned that Conley did not admit he knew a crime had taken place before he wrote the notes which meant that Frank had dictated the notes arbitrarily.

Pencil company officials responded that they believed that Conley was at the plant to rob one or more employees, however, police disputed this and never followed up. Phagan's purse was never found, but again Police refused to follow up on the possibility that Conley robbed the girl and took the purse since he was an important witness against Frank who everyone knew was the killer.

The police attempted to arrange a face to face meeting between Frank and Conley, but Frank wanted his attorney present who was out of town. As a result, the meeting did not take place. The *Atlanta Constitution* quoted police as saying Frank's refusal to meet without his attorney present proved he was guilty.

Determined to finalize the case against Frank, on May 29th, police met with Conley for over four hours. During this meeting, Conley agreed to prepare a new affidavit. In this third affidavit, Conley admitted that he had previously lied. He now said that Frank told him that *he had picked up a girl back there and let her fall and that her head hit against something*. Conley now said that he and Frank took the body to the basement via the elevator and then returned to Frank's office where Frank dictated the murder notes.

According this this third affidavit, and fourth statement, the two returned to Frank's office where Conley hid in the wardrobe. He also said that Frank had given him $200.00, but took it back, saying that *"Let me have that and I will make it all right with you Monday if I live and nothing happens."* At the trial, Conley changed his story again and said that Frank withheld the $200.00 until Conley had burned the body in the basement furnace.

The *Georgian* hired William Manning Smith to represent Conley for the sum of $40.00. Smith believed that Conley had told the truth in his fourth statement, but he was concerned that Conley was giving long jailhouse interviews to the media. He had him moved to another wing of the jail and no one was able to get to him except officers. On February 14, 1914, Conley was sentenced to a year in jail for being an accomplice after the fact to the murder of Mary Phagan.

THE TRIAL

Frankly, the verdict from the trial was almost a foregone conclusion. The Atlanta Constitution, which had broken the story, the Atlanta Journal and the Atlanta Georgian, were competing to see which paper could publish the most lurid details of this murder. The newspaper coverage combined real evidence leaked form police with unsubstantiated rumors and blatant speculation. The public ate it up. By the time of the trial, there was no one qualified to sit on the jury who had not been made aware of every single aspect of the case. Naturally, the papers had been daily trying Frank in the press to the point that the public called him that Jewish Pervert. How could he get a fair trial?

On May 23, 1913, a grand jury was convened to hear evidence for an indictment against Leo Frank for the murder of Mary Phagan. Hugh Dorsey, the Prosecutor presented only enough evidence to obtain the indictment, assuring the jury that he had additional evidence that would be presented at trial. ON May 24th, the Grand Jury returned an indictment. Frank's legal team demanded that the Grand Jury indict Jim Conley, as they were sure he was the actual killer. The Grand Jury foreman, on his own authority convened the jury on July 21th, but Hugh Dorsey convinced the jury not to indict Conley. After all, he was the State's star witness.

The trial began on July 28 in the Fulton County Superior Court. Leonard S. Roan was the judge. The prosecution team was a little unusual. Hugh Dorsey was the Prosecutor assisted by William Smith, Jim Conley's attorney. Leo Frank was defended by a team of eight attorneys. In addition to the hundreds of spectators inside the courtroom, there were thousands gathered outside the building. This tremendous crowd and all of the media pressure for a conviction was one of the factors brought out in later appeals as factors in the alleged intimidation of the witnesses and the jury.

The prosecution presented witness who testified as to the hair and bloodstains found on the lathe in the metal room to support their theory that the murder took place on the 2nd floor of the factory, near Frank's office[30]. There was much argument as to where the murder took place, in spite of the testimony as to the blood stains. Certainly, the cord tied around her neck could be found throughout the factory.

The Prosecution believed that the scene in the basement supported Conley's story (remember, the assistant Prosecutor was Conley's own attorney, a clear conflict of interest that the Court ignored), that the body was carried down on the elevator[31]. However, the drag marks, which police had not thoroughly investigated, supported the idea that the body was taken down the ladder and then drug across the floor.

---

[30] From the records there seemed to be an assumption that the hair and blood found on the lathe belonged to Mary Phagan. However, there was no evidence presented that it was actually hers.
[31] The implication was that only Frank had the key to the elevator.

Then there was the purse, which still had not been found. Prior to the trial and in his various statements, Conley denied knowing anything about the purse. However, at trial, and after careful police coaching, he said that he saw Frank put the purse in his office safe. Of course, when the safe was opened on Monday after the murder, there was no sign of the missing purse.

Now the sexual aspects of the case came to the forefront. The Prosecution alleged that Frank, with Conley's assistance, regularly met with women in his office for sexual relations. In another change to his previous statements, Conley now said that he saw Phagan go upstairs and heard a scream shortly after that. He said that he dozed off and when he awoke, Frank called him upstairs and showed him Phagan's body. He said that Frank admitted that he had hurt Mary and then he reverted to his previous statements about taking the body to the basement.

The defense cross examined Conley for sixteen hours, but they were unable to break his story. The defense then moved to have his testimony stricken in its entirety concerning the alleged rendezvous. Judge Road ruled that had the objection been made earlier, he might have agreed, but since the testimony had been made, it could not be unheard by the jury, so he denied the objection.

The Prosecution then addressed the issue of whether or not Frank expected Mary to come to his office that Saturday. They called Helen Ferguson, the factory worker who had first notified Mary's parents of her murder[32]. Ferguson testified that she had tried to pick up Phagan's pay on Friday from Leo Frank but was told that Phagan would have to come pick it up in person. According to the prosecution, this proved that Frank had reason to expect Mary to come to his office on Saturday.

---

[32] No one, as far as the record indicates, ever inquired as to how Helen Ferguson found out that Mary had been murdered when it seemed no one else knew.

However, two witnesses, both the person who manned the pay window and the woman standing behind Ferguson in the line at the pay window disputed her testimony. Both said that in accordance with normal practice, Frank did not disburse the pay that day and that it was common practice that no one could pick up someone else's pay envelope unless prior arrangements had been made. The Prosecution discounted this testimony.

The defense also called a number of factory girls who testified that they had never seen Frank flirting with or touching the girls, and that they considered him to be a person of good character. In rebuttal, Dorsey called a steady stream of former factory workers and asked the question, *"Do you know of Mr. Frank's character for lasciviousness?"* The answers were usually negative. Hearsay, with no evidence to support it, but accepted by the court.

VERDICT

There were numerous charges and counter-charges between the defense and the prosecution regarding witness tampering, intimidation and bribery. The Defense went so far as to request a mistrial dur to their belief that the jury had been intimidated by the mass crowds surrounding the Courthouse, but the motion was denied. However, fearing for the safety of Frank and his lawyers in case he was found not guilty, Judge Roan and the defense team agreed that neither Frank nor his attorneys would be present when the verdict was read.

On August 25, 1913, after less than four hours of deliberation, the jury reach what was said to be a unanimous guilty verdict. Leo Frank was guilty of murder. It is also interesting to note that even though Jury deliberations are supported to be secret, the very next morning, the Atlanta Journal reported that the deliberations took less than two hours. The first ballot showed that one juror was undecided, but within two hours, a second ballot was unanimous for guilty. It would seem that the news media had a direct pipeline to the jury room.

On August 26, 1913, the day after the guilty verdict was read, Judge Roan brought counsel into his private chambers and sentenced Leo Frank to death by hanging, setting the date for October 10th. The defense team immediate issued a public protest claiming that public opinion and news reports unconsciously influenced the jury against Frank.

At this time, under Georgia law, appeals of death penalty cases had to be based on errors of law, not a reevaluation of the evidence. The appeals process had to begin with a reconsideration by the trial judge. The defense presented a written appeal alleging 115 procedural issues. On October 31, 1913, Judge Roan denied the motion stating that while he was not thoroughly convinced that Frank was guilty or innocent, he didn't have to be convinced, the jury did have to be convinced and it was clear that they were.

The next step in the appeals process was a hearing before the Georgia Supreme Court. In addition to raising the previous arguments, the defense also focused on Judge Roan's stated reservations. They also cited six cases where new trials had been granted after the trial judge expressed misgivings about the jury verdict. The Prosecution countered with arguments that the evidence convicting Franks was substantial[33] and that listing the Judge's doubts in the defense's Bill of Exception was not the proper way to present this evidence. On February 7, 1914, in a 142-page decision, the Georgia Supreme Court denied Frank a new trial. However, the dissenting Justices restricted their opinion to Conley's testimony which they declared should not have been allowed to stand. They concluded that the

---

[33] This substantial evidence was primarily Conley's coached four affidavits.

evidence prejudiced Frank in the juror's eyes and denied him a fair trial. In spite of this, on March 7, 1914, Frank's execution was set for April 17, 1914.

In spite of these losses, the defense did not give up. Based on their discoveries, they filed an extraordinary motion before the State Supreme Court. This resulted in a stay of execution and the hearing on this extraordinary motion opened on April 23, 1914. The defense had amassed a mountain of new evidence that called the verdict into question.

A number of witnesses wrote affidavits that repudiated their testimony. A State biologist ran tests on the hairs found on the lathe and stated in a newspaper interview that the hairs did not match those of Mary Phagan. This newly amassed evidence was leaked to the media and as a result the state began to seek repudiations of the repudiations. An analysis of the murder notes showed that they had probably been written in the basement and not in Frank's office as stated by Conley in his testimony.

There was one other issue regarding the police investigation that was revisited at this point in the appeals process. During the initial investigation, undisturbed human excrement was found in the bottom of the elevator shaft. When question, Conley admitted that he had left it there before the murder. On Monday after the murder when authorities used the elevator, it crushed the excrement. This meant that if Frank and Conley had used the elevator on Saturday to transport the body as claimed by Conley, it would have crushed the excrement, but it was undisturbed when police found it after the murder.

Dorsey responded that this proved nothing as the elevator did not always go all the way to the bottom, it could be stopped anywhere. However, Conley, himself, had stated that it always went to the bottom. During a request to

Governor Slaton[34] for a commutation of the sentence, the Governor conducted his own tests and discovered that the elevator always went to the bottom of the shaft, thus Conley lied about he and Frank transporting the body to the basement in the elevator. It was also discovered that the notes were written on dated order pads that had been signed by a previous employee and that they were only kept in the basement. So, the notes had not been written in Frank's office as Conley claimed.

Based upon all of the clear problems with the trial, Governor Slaton commuted Frank's death sentence to life imprisonment on Monday, June 21, 1915. In response, Atlanta Mayor, Jimmy Woodward commented to the press that the larger part of the population believes that Frank is guilty and that the commutation was a mistake.

---

[34] Slaton was an attorney and his firm had merged with that of Frank's defense counsel. So many felt that Slaton was biased. No one cared at this point out the evidence.

The public was outraged over Slaton's actions. A mob threatened to attack the Governor at his home. A detachment of the Georgia National Guard, county policemen and a group of Slaton's friends who had been sworn in as deputies were needed to disperse the mob. For his own protection, Frank was moved to Milledgeville State Penitentiary in the middle of the night for his own safety.

On July 17, the New York Times reported that a fellow inmate by the name of William Creen tried to kill Frank by slashing his throat with a 7-inch butcher knife. When questioned, the attacker told authorities that he wanted to keep the other inmates safe from mob violence, Frank's presence was a disgrace to the prison and he was sure he would be pardoned if he killed Frank.

The June 21, 1915 commutation of Frank's sentence provoked Tom Watson into advocating for Frank's lynching. He claimed that lynch law was a good sign as it showed that a sense of justice lived among the people.

In response a group of 28 prominent men organized themselves into what was called the "Knights of Mary Phagan." These 28 possessed various skills from an electrician to a lay preacher. They openly planned to break Frank out of prison and lynch him.

Now the ringleaders of this group were very well known. However, such is the clannishness and secrecy in Georgia that this list was not published until 200 when Mary Phagan's great niece Mary Phagan Kean posted a list on the web. Among those on this list were Joseph Mackey Brown, former governor of Georgia, Eugene Herbert Clay, former mayor of Marietta and later president of the Georgia Senate; E. Dobbs, mayor of Marietta at the time, Moultrie McKinney Sessions, lawyer and banker, part of the Marietta delegation at Governor Slaton's clemency hearing, several current and former Cobb county Sheriffs and a number of other prominent civic leaders.

On the afternoon of August 16, eight cars carrying the lynch mob left Marietta for Milledgeville. They arrived at the prison about 10:00 PM. The member of the mob that was an electrician cut the phone wires, other members drained the gasoline from the prison's automobiles, handcuffed the warden, and took Frank from his cell in his night shirt and drove away.

The almost seven-hour trip back to Milledgeville was carried out on backroads[35], with lookouts stationed in each small town they had to pass through to make sure that there was no interference. The lynch mob stopped at a place called Frey's Gin, located about two miles east of Marietta. The site had already been prepared with a rope and a table furnished by former Sheriff William Frey. Frank was handcuffed, his legs tied at the ankles and he was immediately hung from a branch of a tree at around 7:00 AM.

---

[35] Top speed of cars in those days was estimated to be 18-20 miles per hour.

The lynch was not a great secret as can be shown by a number of prominent people who were present according to the *Atlanta Journal*. According to the story, a crowd of men, women and children arrived on foot, in cars and on horseback. Souvenir hunters even cut away pieces of Frank's night shirt. According to a *New York Times* story, Robert E. Howell, a relative of Clark Howell, editor of the Atlanta Constitution, tried to whip up the mob to cut the body into pieces, burn it and then bury the remains. Judge Newt Morris tried to restore order and ask for a vote on whether the body should be returned to the parent intact.

A grand jury was empaneled to indict the lynch mob, but no one would testify as to the identity of the members. So as a result of a clear case of murder, no one was punished since it had been done for a good cause. Typical Georgia justice.

This was a clear case of abuse of process, and what amounted to a fixed trial. To make their case, officers suborned perjury, resorted to the third degree and ignored the evidence to convict the man they KNEW was the killer. Leo Frank never saw justice while a live and is still denied justice today. The real killer escaped having to answer for his crimes.

CHAPTER SIX
THE MURDER OF NORA FULLER

It was the year 1902, the city was San Francisco, which even then was something of a melting pot for immigrants of all races and classes. It was also a time when many children were forced to forego what we would call a normal childhood and enter the labor force doing whatever job they possibly could. Such was the case with Eleanor "Nora" Fuller.

Nora, originally born in China, was fifteen years old that fateful year when she was forced to drop out of school to earn a living and held her mother and three siblings. The previous year had not been an easy one for the little family, the parents had recently divorced and the five of them were having to make it on just what the mother could bring in. For this reason, Nora decided to help out.

Nora had wanted to try and make a go of it in the theater and had made inquiries at an agency to try and find employment related to this field. However, on January 8, 1902, another opportunity came her way that she could not resist.

She saw an advertisement in the San Francisco Chronicle which read "*Wanted – Yong white girl to take care of baby; good home and good wages.*"

Hoping for at least a chance to interview, Nora answered the ad and shortly received a postcard in reply. The post card instructed her to meet a man named John Bennett at the Popular Restaurant at 55 Geary Street at either 1:00 PM or 6:00 PM.

On the day set for the meeting, January 11th, Nora left her home about 5:00 PM for her appointment. The next thing heard from the young woman was a telephone call to her home that was answered by her 12-year-old brother. Nora informed him that she was John Bennett's residence at 1500 Geary Street. She had been offered the job of caring for the baby and her employer wanted her to start work at once. Nora's mother came on the line and insisted that she come home and start her job on Monday. Nora agreed and hung up. That was the last that anyone heard from Nora.

Even though Nora did not come home that evening as she had been instructed to do, surprisingly her mother did not report her as missing for several more days. It must be said though that once she was reported as missing, the San Francisco police immediately went to work trying to find the young woman. Based upon what Nora's mother told them, officers first went to the Popular Restaurant where Nora was to have had the meeting with John Bennett.

The owner of the restaurant, F.W. Krone, told officers that at around 5:30 PM on January 11, a man had come to the counter to let him know that he was expecting a young girl to come in looking for John Bennett and to please send her to his table. As the man was recognized as a regular by both the owner as well as a longtime waiter, no one thought anything of the request. In fact, upon more thorough questioning, both swore that the man had been dining there regularly for at least a decade, though neither had known his name until that day.

The owner swore that he had not seen the girl come into the restaurant, though he could not say that she had not. However, he could say that John Bennett waited for about half an hour, after which he had gone outside and paced impatiently for a few minutes before leaving. John Bennett was described as being about 40 years old, of average height and weight, with brown hair and a brown moustache. He presented a smart and respectable appearance.

Officers who went to 1500 Geary Street, the address that Nora had given her brother in the telephone call. They discovered that this was not a valid address as it was merely a vacant lot. Since Nor had allegedly called her home from this address, the question now arose, had Nora lied and if so, why?

For the next month, there was extensive newspaper coverage regarding what was being called the Nora Fuller case. It was splashed across the front pages of all of the San Francisco papers, but in spite of a citywide manhunt, no trace of the young girl was ever turned up. In addition, there was absolutely no trace of the mysterious John Bennett found as well.

However, this was to change. On the afternoon of February 8th, H.E. Dean, an inspector and a rent collector for real estate firm of Umbsen & Company entered a rented property located at 2211 Suter Street in San Francisco. The residence was locked, and it was clear that no one was at home, so Dean had used a pass key to enter the premises.

Entering by way of a passkey was not a normal practice, but the rent was due, and Umbsen & Company had been informed that the tenants had moved out. The house had been rented only a month earlier by a C.B. Hawkins, but all attempts to contact him had been in vain. So, it was that H.E. Dean was sent to check on things.

AS soon as he entered the premises, H.E. Dean knew that something was not right. There was not a stick of furniture on the entire first floor. He went from room to room and found there was not a single indication that anyone had been there in some time. Having finished his inspection of the first floor, Dean slowly climbed the stairs to the second floor.

He went slowly down the second-floor hallway checking each room that he came to, only to see that each was empty. Finally, he noticed that the door to one of the back bedrooms was closed tightly. Slowly, cautiously, he opened that closed door to see that the room was in darkness, all of the shades drawn down to the very bottom of the windows. He was just able to make out that there were pieces of clothing strewn about the floor of the room.

He did not venture any further into the dim bedroom, sensing that something was not quite right. Deciding that caution was the better part of valor, Dean pulled the door softly closed and retreated to the street, returning with Police Officer Gill. Together they went back up the stairs, pausing just outside that closed bedroom door.

Taking the lead, Officer Gill cautiously entered the dimly lit bedroom, crossing to the closest window. He raised the shade and turned toward the only piece of furniture in the room, a large bed. To his horror lying spread-eagled on the bed was a young girl. She was clearly dead and her body was partially decomposed.

At that point, Officer Gill left the room, closing the door behind him. With Dean in tow, he left the house to summon detectives. After an initial examination, it was determined that the dead body was that of the missing Nora

Fuller, she had been raped and strangled. Her body had been savagely mutilated.

A thorough search of the property revealed one towel, a mostly empty bottle of whiskey, the butt of a cigar and several pieces of junk mail addressed to Mrs. C.B. Hawkins of 221 Sutter Street. One of the pieces of junk mail had been opened and stuffed into the pocket of Nora Fuller's jacket. Her purse as also found but it contained neither money nor the postcard that had led her to meet John Bennett.

Further investigation revealed that the bed was secondhand and had been bought the day after the house had been rented as had the sheets, the pillows and the quilt. The bedding had been placed on the bed straight out of the packaging without the benefit of being laundered first. The only other furniture in the entire house was a single chair that had also been purchased second hand.

Further forensic examination showed that Nora had some alcohol in her system and that the last thing she had eaten was an apple, which had been eaten, it was estimated on an hour or two before her death. Nora's mother said that Nora had eaten an apple just before setting out for her appointment. This of course led authorities to believe she had been murdered almost immediately after arriving at the house.

Police believed that the man known as John Bennett and the man who rented the house as C.B. Hawkins were probably the same man. A canvass of secondhand shops in the area confirmed that a man fitting Bennett's description had purchased pieces of furniture and bedding only a few days before Nora's disappearance. They all said that the deliveries were made to 2211 Sutter Street.

This information called into question the initial assumption that Nora had been killed immediately. Why go to all of the trouble of renting a house and buying furniture if the plan was to kill her immediately?

As if things were not confusing enough, a friend of Nora's came forward with a new twist to the mystery. According to Madge Graham, Nora had been secretly dating an older man by the name of John Bennett for some time. Madge went on to say that she had even covered for Nora by telling Nora's mother that she and Nora were at the theater when in actuality, Nora was out with Bennett.

Madge also claimed that the ad for the nanny job was actually a ruse to fool Mrs. Fuller into thinking that Nora was applying for a job as a nanny when she really intended to meet her much older boyfriend. While the entire concept that Nora would go to the trouble and expense of placing an ad and then answering it boggled the imagination, it would explain why Nora gave her brother the wrong address. Of course, the placing of the ad did tend to be an extreme method of getting time to meet a man and ads were not cheap by any means even in 1902.

Madge's story received some support when a grocer by the name of A. Menke came forward to reveal that Nora often came into his store to use the phone to call a nearby hotel when her family had a phone at home. Perhaps she was calling her mysterious older boyfriend

The police were somewhat suspicious of Madge Graham's story, nevertheless, but then a new lead came to light that indirectly supported Madge's story. On January 18th, a week after Nora's disappearance and three weeks before her body was found, police had received a report that a man by the name of Charles B. Hadley, clerk at the *San Francisco Examiner*, had allegedly embezzled a large sum of money from his employers and vanished.

In investigating this embezzlement case, police talked to Hadley's girlfriend, Ollie Blasier. She had a few interesting things to say. She gave police samples of

Hadley's handwriting which bore a marked resemblance, not only to John Bennett's handwriting on the classified ad form he had submitted to the *San Francisco Chronicle*, but also to the handwriting of C.B. Hawkins n the rental agreement for the house at 2211 Suter Street. So now the question was, could the missing Charles B. Hadley actually be John Bennett as well as C.B. Hawkins?

Ollie Blasier also told police that Hadley had a particular fondness for tenderloin[36], that he had seemed oddly disturbed upon reading in the newspaper that Nora Fuller had been murdered and that she had found blood on a few pieces of his clothing around the time it was believed that Nora had been murdered. She also added, as an afterthought that though Hadley was clean shaven, he sometimes worse a false moustache.

---

[36] This fact referenced information received form the owner of the restaurant that John Bennett would always order a porterhouse steak and then only eat the tenderloin portion.

Further investigation also revealed that Charles B. Hadley was actually Charles Start who was wanted for another charge of embezzlement in Minneapolis in 1889 and that he had also allegedly raped another fifteen-year-old girl in San Francisco in 1900.

So now the question became who was Charles Start and was he really the killer of fifteen-year-old Nora Fuller? In spite of a nationwide manhunt, Hadley, or whatever his name might be was never found. This case leads to several questions that as yet are not answered:

- Was the body on the bed really that of Nora Fuller?
- When and how did she actually die?
- How long had she been dead when her body was found?
- If John Bennett was Nora's boyfriend, why did he ask the owner of the restaurant to direct the girl that would ask for him to his table?
- Who was Nora calling at the nearby hotel?

Even assuming that Nora was planning to set up housekeeping with an unknown man, there was no proof that it was Hadley, or Bennett or whatever his name may have been. This was a case for forensic evidence if there ever was one.

CHAPTER SEVEN
THE DEATH OF LITLE LORD FAUNTLEROY

On March 8, 1921, the body was a young boy, estimated to be between five and seven years old was fished out of a pond near the O'Laughlin Stone Company by one John Brlich. The initial examination suggested that the child had been killed by a blow to the head with a blunt object and had been in the water for some time. It was also determined that the child had brown eyes and blonde hair. From his clothing it was believed that the child's parents had money.

Due to the child's apparel, the investigators called the boy "Little Lord Fauntleroy." Since the assumption was that the boy's parents were affluent, it was assumed that this case would be quickly solved, as least in so far as the child's identify was concerned. But such was not to be the case.

Though detailed descriptions of the dead child were immediate circulated no one came forward to claim the body. Police even displayed the body at the local funeral home for several days, but no one appeared concerned about the child. Then a $1,000.00 reward was posted for any information about the boy's identity, but still no one came forward with any information.

There was only one clue that came forward. An employee of the O'Laughlin Stone Company reported that a couple had come to the business office a month before the child's body was found and asked if anyone had seen a little boy in the area. They seemed very upset. The man was seen to scan the area around the quarry carefully as though looking for something. Finally, the couple drove off. The employee failed to get their license number, so it was impossible for the authorities to find them.

There was speculation that the dead boy had been kidnapped for ransom. If this was the case, it was believed that the kidnappers may have told the parents that their child would be near the quarry. Of course, if this was the case, why didn't the parents go to the police?

Then there was a report that the woman that had asked about the child had committed suicide by jumping into the quarry where the boy's body had been found. However, a thorough search of the quarry by the police revealed no woman's body.

Then there was the report that came from a man from Chicago by the name of J.B. Belson. He thought that the child might be his nephew and that the child might have been murdered by his sister's ex-husband. Police investigated this lead thoroughly before deciding that it led nowhere.

A local woman from Waukesha by the name of Minnie Conrad raised the money to bury the child and even took care of his grave until her own death. However, as an interesting side note, there have been numerous reports over the years that another woman who face was always concealed behind a veil would come and leave flowers on Little Lord Fauntleroy's grave. She has never been identified. To date, the real identity of the dead child has never been determined, but I would suggest that with today's interest in genealogy and the DNA data bases that are available, his relatives could be easily found.

CHAPTER EIGHT
THE ATLANTA RIPPER

Atlanta, Georgia has been the scene was a lot of bloody murders, but the story of the Atlanta Ripper is unusual in the length of time this killer prowled the streets of this city without being apprehended. Interestingly, this case did not receive much in the way of publicity outside the city as the victims of the fiend known as the Atlanta Ripper were members of the Black Community. Then, as now, in Georgia, issues in the Black community tended to stay in the Black community.

These killing actually appear to have begun in the year 1909 but there was no clear evidence that attributed every one of these killings to the same individual. Actually, the police never really pursued the idea of the Atlanta

Ripper, believing that there was no such thing. However, the circumstances of each killing seemed to show a decided relationship to each other, making it likely it was one person.

The first killing that was probably committed by the Atlanta Ripper took place in the year 1909. In April of that year the body of Della Reid was discovered in a trash pile. In September of that year, a female victim who has never been identified was pulled out of Peachtree Creek. She had been stabbed and her throat cut.

The series of murders that many people feel were actually committed by the Atlanta Ripper continued through the year 1910. In addition to the two listed above there were seven others. Of course, researchers have argued that these seven murders may not have been committed by the Ripper since, all but one, was shot. They could have simply been the victims of domestic violence or other circumstances that led to their murders. Certainly, it is not beyond the realm of possibility that these women were in fact Ripper victims, but he simply had changed his methods of killing.

Many who have written about this time period have pointed to the clear institutionalized racism that existed in Atlanta. It was only three years before the first murder when there were massive race riots in Atlanta in which 25 African Americans were killed by white mobs following a series of accusations that they were raping white women. Many of these accusations were later proven to be false, but that did not bring back those killed during the riots.

It was also true that during this time period, in spite of claims of tolerance and progress in Atlanta that were made by the Mayor of Atlanta and the Governor of Georgia, the Jim Crow laws were still on the books, Black voters were still faced with a poll tax that literally disenfranchised them and police investigators generally paid little attention to crimes committed in the Black community.

It was not until 1910 that it began to become clear to even the most myopic city leader that the evidence supported the idea that that it was a single individual who was committing these murders. A detailed study of the evidence, when prejudice was put aside, that these murders all showed the hallmarks of a woman hating psychopath in the vein of Jack the Ripper who terrorized London in the 1880s.

The murderer that seemed to gain the full attention of the Atlanta police took place on October 3, 1910. That morning the body of a 23-year-old cook by the name of Maggie Brooks was discovered. Her head had been bashed in with a rock or some such similar weapon. As time went on, it became clear to police that this bashing in of the skull was a trademark for the murders that happened later. It was the trademark, so to speak, of the Atlanta Ripper.

Of course, at the time, police still had not come to understand that this was the work of serial killer. When one looks at the cases individually and not as a whole, patterns are very hard to spot. Frankly, with the murder rate in the Black community in the early 1900s, the Ripper could have started killing before 1909, but this fact will never be confirmed due to the desire of authorities not to open old wounds or further embarrass themselves for their failure to miss the signs of a serial killer.

However, at the time, since there were no more unexplained murders of Black women for the balance of the year, it was business as usual. The on January 22, 1911, thirty-five-year-old Rosa Trice was found with her skull caved in and her throat was slashed. Evidence showed that her body was been dragged to where it was found, only a hundred yards from her own doorstep. In a typical myopic knee-jerk reaction, police immediately arrested her husband John Trice for the murder. Case closed. Well, until they had to release him for lack of evidence, that it.

In hind sight, Rosa Trice's murder became the templet against which other Ripper murders were compared.

The Ripper's modus operandi was to approach a woman on the street, bash her in the head and drag her body to a more secluded spot where he could take his time with her. Generally, this meant that the victim was stabbed and mutilated before her throat was finally slashed. Another peculiar action by the Ripper was to cut the women's shows off their feet and take them with him.

In early February Lucinda McNeal was murdered with a straight razor. Immediately there were those who believed that the Ripper had struck again. However, in typical fashion, the police immediately arrested the husband based on some witness statements that Lucinda had been killed by her husband in a drunken rage. Charles McNeal was tried and convicted of her murder, getting a life sentence in prison. Like finding a needle in a haystack, the police were dealing with too many crimes to be able to get the big picture, not that the murder of Black women was given major attention.

The next actual Ripper murder took place on February 18, 1911. This time, the scene of the crime was just past the Atlanta City Limits which meant that the Atlanta Police were not the primary investigative agency. It also meant that they basically ignored the case. However, be that as it may, the murdered woman, who is still unidentified to this day, appeared to be about 25 years old. Her skull was smashed in, though there was no mention in media reports of her throat being slashed. It was interesting to note that the killer took his time with her as there were empty beer bodies strewn around the body.

On April 5, 1911, Georgia Brown was found dead. Since she was shot and not bashed in the head, most people do not believe she was the victim of the Atlanta Ripper. However, whether she was or was not will never be known as her murder was never solved.

The next murder that was probably committed by this unknown killer took place on Mary 27, 1911. Though there had been a fairly lengthy period of time between murders to this point, something changed. The murder that took place on Mary 27th seemed to be the beginning of a series of crimes committed by this creature of the shadow. Mary 27th, Mary "Belle" Walker was a cook. She was walking home from her job on this Saturday night and apparently came face to face with the mysterious Ripper. She was found dead the next morning, her throat had been slashed.

On June 15th, the next victim was added to the list. Her name was Addie Watts. She was found with her skull smashed in with a brock. Her body had then been drug into some shrubbery where she was beaten in the head with a train coupling pin. As a final indignity, her throat was slashed.

On June 24th, another Black woman by the name of Lizzie Watts was murdered. She had been hit in the head, drug into some nearby bushes and her throat had been sashed.

Though the police maintained that they had begun to suspect a serial killer was at work, it appears that it was an enterprising newspaper reporter who actually noticed the pattern. Until the papers started asking if there was a killer on the loose, the stories of the murder of Black women, if they were reported at all, were related to the back pages with little detail. It was assumed that the killings were simple the product of the degeneracy to be found in the Black community and certainly initially, no one in their right mind assumed that one person was committing these murders.

In fact, in response to the suggestion that there was a single killer, so resistant were some authorities to the idea of one killer that it was claimed that this was a convenient and fictional scapegoat for men to use to cover up the murder of their wives or girlfriends.

On July 1st another attack took place, but the purported second victim of the night managed to survive and gave a brief description of her attacker. On this Saturday night, twenty-year-old Emma Lou Sharpe was sitting at home waiting for her mother to return from the grocery store. Finally, concerned it was taking her other so long to return, Emma Lou began to walk to the grocery to see why her mother was so late.

Emma Lou arrived at the grocery only to be told that he mother had never been there. With no idea what to do, or where else to look for her mother Emma Lou decided to return home. On the way there she was approached in the street by a tall, broad-shouldered black man wearing a wide brimmed hat. Beside herself with worry, she was not really paying attention when the man spoke to her. He asked her how she was feeling. She was baffled by the question but answered fine and tried to keep walking, however, he stepped in front of her and blocked her path.

Now, concerned for her own safety, she tried to get around the man. As she brushed past him, she heard him say

"Don't be afraid. I never hurt girls like you." In the next breath he then stabbed her in the back as e reached for her.

Feeling the knife entering her back, Emma Lou screamed at the top of her lungs and took off running as fast as she could, blood running down her back. Luckily, some neighbors heard her screams and came running to her assistance. The mysterious black man in the wide brimmed hat stopped chasing her and seemingly vanished back into the shadows from whence he had come.

Her mother was not as lucky as Emma Lou. Neighbors, who were searching for Emma Lou's attacker, found her mother's body in some nearby bushes. She had been hit in the head and her throat had been slashed.

On July 10th, workmen on Atlanta Avenue noticed a trial of blood leading into a small gully. Deciding to follow the blood trail, the men found the body of Sadie Holley. Her head had been bashed in with a rock, which was found lying nearby, her throat had been slashed and her shoes had been cut off of her feet. Bloodhounds were brought in to try and track the killer, but they lost the scent after about 200 yards.

The crime scene contained all of the classic trademarks of the Atlanta Ripper, but the police preferred to rely on the tried and true methods of solving crime. Find someone to arrest, anyone, it really didn't matter.

The next day, they arrested a man by the name of Henry Huff and charged him with Sadie's murder. A witness claimed that he had seen Huff with Sadie on the night of the murder and that they had been arguing. Additionally, police claimed that Huff had been found with dirt and blood on his clothes. As a result of this witness's unsupported word, Huff was held on suspicion and eventually indicted, though it appeared that no one, not even the police, really believed that Huff was guilty. But the police could now brag they had caught the killer, which removed some of the pressure on them from the leaders of the Black community.

At the same time as police arrested Henry Huff, they also arrested another man that witnesses said had been seen with Sadie. This man was named Todd Henderson. There were some sources that claimed that Emma Lou Sharpe had identified Henderson as the man that had stabbed her in the back, but others said that she could not be sure.

To put some icing on the cake, so to speak, police also arrested and indicted a third suspect, John Daniel. Though everyone was assured that the killings were at an end with all of the arrests, no one seemed really confident that the Atlanta Ripper had been caught.

In spite of these assurances, on August 31st, there was another murder that revealed the same trademarks as the earlier killings. The victim was twenty-year-old Mary Ann Duncan. Her body was found lying on the railroad tracks on the west side of Atlanta. Her throat had been slashed and her shoes cut of her feet.

October 21st, another victim was found. Her name was Eva Florence and her head had been bashed in and her throat slashed. Everything about this murder screamed Ripper.

In November, another victim was discovered. Her name was Minnie Wise and she was hit in the head with a rock and her body was found dumped on a trash heap where two previous victims had been found. Her throat was slashed, and her right index finger was cut off at the joint. Naturally, police immediately suspected that her husband, Bud Wise had killed her and simply made it look like a Ripper murder, but this was never proven. At this point police would have arrested the Eastern Bunny to keep form admitting that there was a serial killer stalking the Black community.

As with so many serial killers, there seems to be a tendency to escalate the horror of the killings. The same was true of the Atlanta Ripper. On November 21st, the still warm body was Mary Putnam was found lying in a ditch, partially covered with loose dirt. Her skull had been crushed, her throat had been slashed. That was enough for it to be viewed as a Ripper murder, but in this case her breast also was slashed open and her heart was torn out of her ribcage and left sitting beside the body. With this gruesome act, the Ripper was believed to have ended his killings for 1911.

During the first few months of 1912, there were five Black women murdered in Atlanta. Unfortunately, due to an absence of records it is impossible to tell how many of these victims were killed by the Ripper.

On January 12, 1912, Ida Ferguson was found stabbed to death. Again, in an immediate knee jerk reaction, Police arrested her boyfriend Lucky Elliot who was later convicted of the murder. All of the evidence against him was circumstantial, but police "knew" he did it, so he had to be convicted.

On Saturday, January 20th, the body of Pearl Williams was found. Her throat had been slashed. Police pointed the finger at Frank Harvey who had told witnesses that he wanted to marry her and if couldn't have her, no one could. The police also arrested a seventeen-year-old by the name of Edgar Evans in regard to this murder, but his involvement was never revealed.

On February 15th, the body of Alacy Owens was found. While some viewed this as another Ripper killing, the police immediately arrested her husband Charles Owens for her murder and he was later convicted based on somewhat sketchy circumstantial evidence.

On April 15th, the body of an unknown fifteen-year-old girl was found. Her throat had been cut and she had been thrown into the river.

On May 11th, an unidentified woman was found who had been hit in the head, dragged into some nearby shrubbery and had her throat slashed.

As far as can be determined, this murder of the unidentified woman on May 11th was the last of the Ripper murders. Some question whether or not all of the murders committed over the two-year period when the Ripper was said to be the most active were actually committed by one man. The unfortunate thing is that due to the large number of crimes committed in the Black community during this time period and the tendency of law enforcement to chalk them up to the degeneracy of the Black race, the investigation never serious addressed the possibility that there was serial killer attacking Black women. A sad commentary on the concept of equal justice for all.

CHAPTER NINE
THE MURDER OF PAT GARRETT

The name Pat Garrett[37] is well known to any student of the old west. He was at one time or another a lawman, a bartender, an author, a Texas Ranger and a customs agent, but he was best known for allegedly killing Billy the Kid. At various times, he served as the sheriff of Lincoln County, New Mexico as well as Dona Ana County, New Mexico. Like many famous personages form the old west, his reported life is a mixture of legend and fact. He was murdered February 29, 1908 under very strange circumstances. His murder is still unsolved today.

---

[37] He name was actually Patrick Floyd Jarvis Garrett.

There are many stories told about Pat Garrett's life and death. He was said to have killed Billy the Kid with a shot to the heart in a darkened room, when there is evidence that Pat Garrett actually faked Bill's death to help his young friend get a fresh start and earn himself $500.00 promised him by Lew Wallace, the territorial governor, in the process[38]. But that is another story.

What is not talked about much is that after he choose not to seek re-election as Sheriff of Lincoln County in 1882, he moved to Texas. On March 10, 1884, Texas governor John Ireland appointed Garrett as a lieutenant in the Texas Ranger. However, in spite of enjoying his duties, within a year, Garrett resigned his commission and returned to his ranch near Roswell, New Mexico.

However, Garrett was not a man who liked to stay in one place for too long. In 1892, he moved his large family to

---

[38] Hudnall, Ken. The Border Escapades of Billy The Kid, Omega Press 2017/

Uvalde, Texas where he became a very close friend to John Nance Garner, a man who would one day be vice president of the United States.

Garrett seemed to be happy in Uvalde, but something happened in New Mexico that drew him back. On January 31, 1896, Colonel Albert Jennings Fountain and his eight-year-old son, Henry, disappeared on the edge of the White Sands area of New Mexico. The mystery of what happened to the Fountains has never been solved. Apache scouts were brought in to try and track the buckboard that Fountain had been driving to no avail, not even Pinkerton Detectives were able to determine what had happened. In April of 1896, Garrett was appointed as sheriff of Dona Ana County to solve the mystery. By 1898, he had collected sufficient evidence to make arrests and asked for warrants for Oliver M. Lee, William McNew, Bill Carr and James Gilliland. It was some months before the four were captured and they were found not guilty at trial.

After Garrett killed his last bad man, a man wanted for murder by the name of Norman Newman, President Theodore Roosevelt[39] nominated Garrett for the post of collector of customs in El Paso, Texas in 1901. He was one of three men known as the Roosevelt's White House Gunfighters[40].

There was a public outcry against his appointment, but Roosevelt was adamant in his determination to appoint Garrett to the position. As a result of Roosevelt's firm support Garrett's appointment was confirmed by the Senate in January 2, 1902. The problem seemed to be that Garrett performed his duties as if he was a sheriff, riding roughshod over many. Then in Mary of 1903, he got into a public fistfight with an employee. Each had to pay five dollars for disturbing the peace. The list of his enemies was growing.

---

[39] DeMattos, Jack, Garrett and Roosevelt, Creative Publishing, College Station, Texas. 1988.
[40] Bat Masterson and Ben Daniels were the other two.

A steady stream of complaints that Garrett was incompetent were sent to Washington, but Roosevelt was firm in his support of Garrett. To further show his support for the former lawman, Roosevelt even invited Garrett to attend a Rough Rider reunion being held in San Antonio. Since Garrett had never been a member of this illustrious group, it was taken as a slap in the face to his critics.

Garett attended the event and even brought a guest of his own who he introduced to the President. This guest was Tom Powers, who Garrett introduced as a cattleman from Texas. Garrett, Powers and Roosevelt were even photographed together and the three sat at the same table for dinner. Garrett's enemies were quick to point that the cattleman from Texas was actually Tom Powers, the owner of a notorious dive in El Paso called the Coney Island Saloon. For Roosevelt this was the last straw, he replaced Garrett with a new collector on January 2, 1906.

Losing his appointment as custom's collector left Garrett in severe financial straits. His ranch near Roswell was heavily mortgaged and when he was unable to make payments, the county auctioned off Garrett's personal possessions in order to satisfy personal judgments against him. The total from the auction game to only $650.00.

With the appointment of George Curry as Territorial Governor of New Mexico by Roosevelt, Garrett thought he saw a way out of his financial problems. He arranged a meeting with Curry who was a long-time friend. Curry promised Garrett that as soon as he was inaugurated as Territorial Governor, he would appoint Garrett to be superintendent of the territorial prison in Santa Fe.

Unfortunately, for Garrett, Curry's inauguration was several months away, and Garret needed money immediately. Leaving his family in New Mexico, Garrett returned to El Paso, Texas where he took a job with the real estate firm, H. M. Maple and Company. He also moved in

UNFINISHED BUSINESS 179

with a woman known to all as Mrs. Brown, who was actually an El Paso prostitute. When word reached Governor-elect George Curry of Garrett's living arrangements in El Paso, he immediately withdrew the offer to be Superintend of the Territorial Prison in Santa Fe, which left Garrett even more desperate that ever.

According to people in the New Mexican town of Oro Grande, after this setback Pat Garrett left El Paso and moved to Oro Grande where he planned to open a store. The building he rented still stands and is looked at as something resembling a museum about Garrett.

At this same time, Dudley Poe Garrett, Pat's son had signed a five-year lease for his Bear Canyon Ranch with Jesse Wayne Brazel. Brazel had said he planned to run cattle on the ranch, but instead brought in a large herd of goats which would ruin the land for cattle grazing for some time. Garrett tried to break the lease due to the goat issue, but more importantly because the money for Brazel's operation had come from his neighbor W.W. Bill Cox and Brazel's partner was going to be Archie Prentice "Print" Rhode, who Garrett despised.

When Brazel refused to terminate the lease, the matter went to court. Attempting to play peacemaker, James B. Miller[41] met with Garrett to try and work out a solution to the problem. After his meeting with Garrett Miller then met with Brazel who agreed to break the lease if someone would by his goat herd. A relative of Miller's by marriage, Carl Adamson agreed to purchase the goat herd of 1,200 goats. But at the last minute, Brazel claimed that he had miscounted and there were actually 1,800 goats rather than 1,200. Adamson refused to purchase that many goats, so the deal fell through. However, later Adamson agreed to meet with Garrett and Brazel to see if they could reach a compromise.

---

[41] James Brown Miller was also known as "Killin Jim", "Killer Miller" and "Deacon Jim". He was a well-known outlaw and professional killer who was said to have killed 12 men during gunfights. He was lynched in Ada, Oklahoma by a mob after assassinating a former deputy U.S. Marshall.

UNFINISHED BUSINESS

According to one story, Garrett and Carl Adamson were riding together form Las Cruces to the meeting. Brazel appeared on horseback along the way and Garrett was shot and killed though who did it and why remains a mystery.

That being said, according to the story told in Oro Grande, Garrett was actually riding into Las Cruces in a buckboard for a meeting and stopped along the roadside to relieve himself as he many times did. As he was in the process of relieving himself, someone stepped from the trees and shot Garrett. His body was left lying alongside the road. It is agreed that both Adamson and Brazel returned to Las Cruces where Brazel is supposed to have told Deputy Sheriff Felipe Lucero that he had killed Garrett.

It does stretch the credulity that Garrett just happened to stop at a place where someone laid in wait for him. It was maintained by those in Oro Grande that Garrett was known to stop at one particular place along the road to relieve himself, so was this a premediated killing? If Brazel was going to make a lot of money selling the goatherd, which was the alleged purpose of the meeting, why would he kill Garrett? Why would a professional assassination such as James Miller get involved as a peacemaker in this disagreement?

Brazel's trial concluded on May 4, 1909. Brazel was represented by Albert Bacon Fall, further Secretary of the Interior. The only eye witness, Carl Adamson was never called as a witness and as a result Brazel was acquitted of Garrett's murder.

For the time, Albert Bacon Fall, very well connected politically, was an expensive attorney. All of Brazel's money was tied up in the goatherd, so who financed his defense? Why was Adamson not called to testify? Was the fix in, insofar as Garrett's murder trial? Whatever may have been the case, for a man like Garrett to be murdered while relieving himself on the side of the road was an ignominious end.

CHAPTER TEN
THE MURDER OF WILLIAM DESMOND TAYLOR

In 1967, Hollywood Director King Vidor took on the job of solving the mystery behind the 1922 murder of director William Desmond Taylor. What he discovered was so explosive that Vidor refused to reveal the identity of the killer.

At the time of the murder, in the early part of 1922, the Murder of William Desmond Taylor was a major scandal in Hollywood. Tinsel Town had already begun to lose some of its glamour as audiences were begining to tire of the silent films that were pouring out of Hollywood and there had been several scandals involving well known stars. Among these were a myriad of stories of excesses and drug use as well as the infamous rape and murder trial of Roscoe "Fatty" Arbuckle[42].

The religious leaders of the day, seeking to increase their own stature at anyone's expense began to clamor for Hollywood to be cleaned up. They thundered form the pulpits about the declining morals of Hollywood and threatened to boycott the movies due to what they called degenerate influences. Certainly, the last thing that the studios needed at this point was another major scandal.

William Desmond Taylor was a well-known name in and among the studios of Hollywood. Originally from Ireland, Taylor, whose real name was William Cunningham Deane-Tanner, had been born into Anglo-Irish gentry on April 26, 1872. He was one of five children of a retired British Army Office and the nephew of Home Rule MP, Charles Kearns Dean Tanner. In 1890, after attending

---

[42] Though the evidence was circumstantial and much of it seemed to prove that Arbuckle had been enticed, his career was ruined as a result of the bad publicity.

Marlborough College in England, Dean-Tanner moved to Kansas but then moved to New York where he married Ethel May Hamilton in 1901. They had a daughter in 1902 or 1903. On October 23, 1908, he vanished from New York, abandoning his wife and daughter. His wife divorced him in 1912.

After wandering the country, Dean-Tanner came to Hollywood in 1912, changed his name, and established a very successful career as an actor and director in silent films. He starred in twenty-seven movies and directed fifty-nine. By 1922, he was a major player in the world of the cinema.

This mystery began on February 1, 1922. William Desmond Taylor was spending a pleasant evening at his home with silent film actress Mabel Normand. According to Miss Normand, the two had enjoyed a quiet evening, chatting, playing the piano and enjoying several illicit cocktails, in spite of the banning of alcohol during Prohibition. She said that around 7:45 PM he had loaned her a book she wanted to read and walked her out to her car. She insisted that nothing out of the way took place.

At approximately 8:00 PM, neighbors heard what they thought was the sound of a car backfiring nearby. In 1922, with the number of early cars found in this affluent neighborhood, a backfiring car was not unusual, just annoying.

A neighbor by the name of Faith McLean, curious about the noise, glanced out a window and saw someone wearing a long coat, scarf and a plaid hat coming out of Taylor's house. This person saw Faith watching, smiled at her and then went back into Taylor's house. It appeared to McLean that this person, who she claimed she did not recognize had forgotten something and return to get it.

Another neighbor by the name of Hazel Gillon also heard the sound of what they all thought was a car backfiring and looked out her window. She also saw what she later described as a dark figure emerge from Taylor's home.

Though she did not recognize the figure, there was nothing that stood out about this unknown person, so she dismissed it and went about her business.

On the morning of February 2, 1922, William Desmond Taylor's assistant Henry Peavy arrived at Taylor's home. As usual, he unlocked the front door and entered ready to start a new day in the movie business. However, when he entered the living room he came to a screeching halt, gaped at what he saw and then ran into the courtyard screaming for help at the top of his lungs. What he had found was William Desmond Taylor lying on his living room floor, very clearly dead.

Once he had calmed down, somewhat, apparently Peavy called Paramount Studios. In those early Hollywood days, the studios controlled everything with an iron fist. The death of a prominent actor/director was certainly something they wanted to be involved in. In fact, it was later found that representatives of the studio arrived at Taylor's home well before the police were even called. While they generally ignored the body, other than making sure that nothing was in his pockets that needed to be removed, they did search the home thoroughly for anything that might reflect badly on Taylor, or Paramount Studios, such as illicit booze, love letters and any other incriminating evidence that they could find. After finishing the search, Harvey Peavy was then assigned to thoroughly clean the house before summoning the police.

No one had any idea how many people actually tracked through the house protecting Paramount Studio's reputation between the discovery of the body and the police arriving. There were several people present when the police investigators did arrive, but no one admitted to removing anything from the home.

Each expressed shock when the police discovered that the death had not been of natural causes, in fact Taylor had been shot in the back with a .38 caliber pistol. By the time the police began their investigation, all that could be determined was that William Desmond Taylor had been murdered sometime the night before and that robbery was not the motive. A search of the body revealed that he had a substantial amount of cash in his pockets and he was wearing a valuable diamond ring on his finger.

After interviewing those in the house and in the surrounding neighborhood, the police arrived at the conclusion that the sound of the car backfiring that several commented on was actually the sound of the shot that killed Taylor. During her interview, Faith McLean also told investigators that the individual she had seen leaving Taylor's home had been what she described as funny looking and appeared to be wearing heavy stage makeup and a classic Burglar costume. She also said that the figure had an effeminate walk. His opened p the possibility that the killer had been a woman disguised as a man.

Mabel Normand was questioned at length since she was apparently the last person other than the killer to see Taylor alive. In fact, she was initially considered to be a suspect, but police could determine neither a motive not any firm evidence that she was the killer. It was determined that he was seeing quite a few women and it was decided that they were more likely suspects than Normand.

Police did discover that there was a possible, and certainly scandalous relationship with actress and former child star Mary Miles Minter[43], who was only 19-years-old at the time of the murder. Everyone knew that Mary Miles Minter was Taylor's protégé, but no one could prove any illicit relationship, though Minter routinely introduced herself as Taylor's fiancé.

The Hollywood tabloids attempted to fabricate a steamy love affair between the two, but those who knew Taylor best claimed that Mary Miles Minter had an

---

[43] Taylor was 49 years old at the time.

obsessive, but unrequited crush on Taylor that he had tried to rid himself of to no avail. She would periodically show up at Taylor's house at all hours clamoring to be let inside so she could be with him.

It was also discovered that Mary Miles Minter was possibly mentally unstable, having one tried to manipulate her family by faking a suicide with a gun approximately 2 years before Taylor's murder. A number of the investigator liked Mary Miles Minter for the killing, theorizing that the person seen by the neighbors at 8:00 PM was not the killer, but that Mary had turned up at Taylor's house much later and threatened to kill herself of Taylor unless he returned her affections.

Of course, the presence of the mystery person at 8:00 PM does raise questions, if Mabel Normand was telling the truth about leaving at about 7:45 PM that night. According to Mabel there were only herself and Taylor in the house until she left in her limo and no one admitted to seeing anyone else arrive. So, how did this mystery person get in the house?

Then there was Mary Miles Minter's mother, Charlotte Shelby, described by all who knew her as a rabid, money-grubbing stage mother, known to be extremely protective of her daughter. It appeared to most that to Charlotte, Mary was much more than a daughter, she was a source of income. If she married, Charlotte would lose control of Mary's fortune. It was reported that she had once pulled a .38 on director Jack Kirkwood and actor Monte Blue when she thought that they were getting too close to her daughter. There had been rumors that both men had indulged in romantic affairs with Mary before she was 19.

Police were especially interested when it was reported that Charlotte had once gone to Taylor's house with a gun threatening to kill him if he did not leave her daughter alone. Those who were familiar with these incidents confirmed that Charlotte's weapon of choice was a .38.

In addition to the female suspects, there were a number of others that police felt had cause to want Taylor dead. He had been working hard to help Mabel Normand kick her addiction to cocaine and he had offered to testify against her suppliers. Certainly, those supplying this star with her drugs felt that Taylor was interfering with something that was none of his business. Based on this, some felt that the killing had been a contract hit.

Police also looked at Henry Peavy, Taylor's assistant and the one who had originally discovered the body. He also had a prior criminal record for lewdness.[44] However, it was finally decided that a much more likely candidate was William's former assistant, Edward Sands[45]. The fact that Taylor never prosecuted Sands was considered a support for the theory that Sands was actually his brother.

---

[44] In Hollywood at the time being accused of lewdness was generally another way of saying one was homosexual.
[45] In the case of Edward Sands, there were a number of rumors that Sands may have actually been Taylor's missing younger brother, Denis Gage Dean-Tanner, but this was never proven.

It was known that Sands had a long rap sheet which included forgery and embezzlement and he was known to also uses a number of aliases and when needed adopt a fake Cockney accent. During his employment by Taylor, he had crashed Taylor's car on a trip to Europe, been caught forging Taylor's name on checks, not to mention being caught stealing expensive items from Taylor's home. He had been let go seven months before the murder and simply vanished.

Primarily due to the meddling of Paramount Studios, complicated by the long list of potential suspects, the Police never had a chance to solve this murder. Though there have been allegations and accusations, no one had ever been charged with the murder of William Desmond Taylor.

It should be noted that as a direct result of the murder of William Desmond Taylor and the other scandals of the 1920s, Hollywood studios required that their actors be bound by moral turpitude clauses in their contracts.

It was rumored that King Vidor discovered the identity of the killer but refused to reveal it, so the case could still be solved with a proper investigation.

CHAPTER ELEVEN
THE CAMDEN TOWN MURDER

The Camden Town Murder took place in 1907. Though this murder took place over twenty years after the last Jack the Ripper Murder, there were many who believed that this murder was either committed by Jack or a very clever copycat.

The victim in this case was one Emily Dimmock, also known to her clients as Phyllis. She was twenty-three years old and was simply trying to make a living on the London streets around Camden Town. She had been born into a poor family in a small village in Hertfordshire. Most of her teenage years were spent working as a maid in various households in the Shire for low wages.

In 1903 or 1904, looking to make her fortune, Emily marshalled her courage, took her small savings and left her home in Hertfordshire moving to London. She found a room in a boarding house, also allegedly a brothel, run by a petty criminal by the name of John William Crabtree. Under his tutelage, she began to ply her trade in what has been called the world's oldest profession, on the streets of London to earn her keep.

She must have been fairly successful because by 1906, she was living in a flat on St. Paul's Road with her 19-year-old common-law husband, Bert Shaw. The couple hoped to get the permission of his parents to marry sometime soon. As a condition of marriage, Emily had promised to give up working as a prostitute and lead a respectful life as a wife and hopefully, soon a mother. Bert was not a wealthy man, but he had a solid steady job as an overnight chef on the Midland Railway.

Though Emily apparently really did long for domestic stability, she had spent the last four years earning her keep on her back, so to speak and it was hard for her to give up her wild restless ways. She missed the drinking in pubs, the bright lights and soliciting men.

Then too, her paramour worked all night, from four-thirty in the afternoon until eleven-thirty in the morning. When he was home, he was tired and wanted to sleep. She was lonely being left all along most of the day and was not getting enough attention. The temptation proved to be too great and she began to step out most evenings without Bert's knowledge. She could be found in the bars along Euston Road.

At one of these bars, the Rising Sun, Emily met a glassware designer by the name of Robert Wood, on or about September 6th. During the investigation, witnesses claimed that Emily and Wood had known each other for a long time while Wood maintained that they had only just met.

The two were sharing a drink at the Rising Sun, that Friday, September 6th. After Emily left, he prepared a postcard on which he wrote "*Phyllis darling, If it pleases you to meet me at 8:15 at the Rising Sun. Yours to a cinder.*" He signed the card Alice to allay any suspicions if the card happened to be seen by Bert Shaw.

Robert Wood apparently mailed this postcard either Sunday or Monday and it arrived at Emily's residence on or before the 11th of September. In the interim, Emily had passed the time entertaining another client by the name of Robert Percival Roberts, a cook. On Wednesday, September 11th, she was seen at the Rising Sun and then at a Bar called the Eagle in the company of Robert Wood.

On Thursday morning, September 12th, at about 11:00 AM, Bert Shaw's mother arrived at her son's home. Most sources later claimed that she had come to give her blessing to the marriage of Emily and Bert. However, there was no answer to Mrs. Shaw's knocks. The landlady of the building in which Bert and Emily had their flat knew Mrs. Shaw and let her into the common area to wait for either Bert or Emily to arrive home. There was no sign of Emily, but Bert arrived home about thirty minutes after his mother arrived.

When Bert and his mother entered the flat, the saw Emily Dimmock naked on the bed, her throat slashed from ear to ear. Blood of her wounds had covered the walls. Forensic examination later determined that she had been murdered in her sleep something between 3:00 AM and 6:00 AM.

The ensuing examination also revealed that though the flat appeared to have been ransacked, nothing had been taken from the flat, except Emily's keys, so that let out robbery as a motive. Most of Emily's postcard collection was scattered over the floor. Two of Bert's straight razors were found next to the sink along with a bloody towel. It appeared that the killer had tried to wash both the razors as well as his hands before leaving the flat and locking up behind him.

When the details of this murder were made public there was a general hue and cry due to the fact that many of the details were similar to those from the Ripper killings. In fact, the media coverage rivaled that given to the Ripper killings in 1888. The story had all of the things that made an editor salivate: a beautiful young victim, lots of sex and many salacious details about the sordid underbelly of London society.

Naturally, suspicion fell almost at once on the glassware designer, Robert Wood. Evidence seemed to prove that he was the last one to see Emily alive. Bert Shaw had come across the postcard that Robert had sent to Emily and once the tabloids published a picture of the card, the handwriting was immediately identified as Robert's by his ex-girlfriend, Ruby Young.

As if this did not cause enough trouble for Robert, Ruby also told police that Robert had come to her and asked her to the authorities that they still saw each other on Monday and Wednesday evenings. Based on this information, and needing to make an arrest, Robert Wood was arrested for the murder of Emily Dimmock.

Frankly, under the prosecution's theory, the case was very straight forward. They claimed that on the evening of Wednesday, September 11, Emily had met Robert Wood as planned at the Rising Sun and then they had gone to the Eagle where they were seen by multiple witnesses. After this, claimed Prosecutors, the couple had gone to Emily's flat where they had sex. Emily fell asleep and, for some unknown reason, Robert killed Emily by slashing her throat. He searched the flat for the postcard he had sent her and failing to find it, he let himself out and locked up with her keys.

The evidence against Robert continued to pour in. Emily's former landlord, John Crabtree came forward to claim that Robert Wood used to visit Emily all of the time when she lived in his boardinghouse. This, of course, contradicted Robert's statement that he had only just met Emily on September 6th. The make matters worse, a number of other witnesses came forward to say that Robert and Emily had been seen together many times prior to the 6th of September.

A neighbor of Emily's by the name of Robert MacCowan claimed that he had seen a man in the street near the Shaw house at a few minutes before 6:00 AM on the morning of the murder. This unknown man had a very odd gait, left hand held stiffly in his pocket, right holder jerking in time with this right foot. According to the authorities, this was the same gait as that of Robert Wood.

All of this evidence coupled with Ruby Young's testimony that Robert tried to use her to manufacture an alibi made his conviction for the murder of Emily Dimmock all but certain.

There is an old saying don't count your chickens before they hatch. The same can be said for murder convictions. The defense raised a number of issues that began to make the case look less than certain as to Robert's guilt. First off, Emily received a letter in the mail. Oddly enough, she burned the letter after reading it. Investigators found only a few scraps when the examined the ashes in the fire place. However, Robert Percival Roberts, another of her clients who had admitted that he had spent three nights with her prior to her death, said that she had shown him the letter before she burned it. It was addressed to Phyllis, her "professional name" and said, *"Will you meet me at the bar of the Eagle in Camden Town 8:30 tonight Wednesday"*. It was signed Bert.

Now Emily's common-law husband was named Bert, but he was never a suspect in her murder. Besides, if he wanted to meet her, he could meet her at home. Finally, at 8:30 in the evening, he was still at work and there was no evidence that he took the night off. So, if Robert Percival Roberts was telling the truth, then one of Emily's men was either named Bert or used Bert as a pseudonym. Besides, if the letter was from her Bert, why would she have burned it in the fire place? There were some that thought since Robert Percival Roberts was a suspect himself, he might have made up the contents of the letter to clear himself, though he did have an alibi.

Robert Wood was represented at trial by one of the most celebrated litigators of that time period, Edward Marshall Hall. He literally tore the prosecution's case to shreds.

In regard to whether or not Robert Wood knew Emily for a long or short period of time, Hall said that Wood simply did not want his ill father to know he was consorting with prostitutes. As to Wood seeing Emily the night she was murdered, that was true, but after spending some time with her at the Eagle, Robert Wood had gong to visit his sick father. A witness testified that Robert Wood arrived at his father's house shortly before midnight and stayed the balance of the night.

As for the testimony of his ex-girlfriend that he had asked her to lie for him to create an alibi, Hall pointed out that it was not for time of the murder, just for the evening. He already had an alibi for the time of the murder.

Hall also established that Wood's gait was not really unusual as several other men with similar gaits could be seen walking the streets every morning. In fact, a boxer by the name of William Westcott came forward to testify that he had a similar gait and had actually been in the area at about 6:00 AM on the day in question and it was probably him that Robert MacCowan had seen and not Robert Wood.

As a final gesture, Robert wood took the stand and those he did not particularly impress the jury, Hall's defense certainly did. It took the jury lass than fifteen minutes to find Wood not guilty. Even the judge gave the opinion that the prosecution had fallen well short of proving their case against Robert Wood.

So now we are back to the question who killed Emily Dimmock? Due to the nature of her profession there could have been ten or a hundred other potential suspects. She could have run into a former client or perhaps it was a new client that killed her.

Many suspected that Robert Percival Roberts was the killer. However, both his friend and his landlady testified that he was in his own flat the entire night of the murder.

During his own testimony, John Crabtree mentioned and individual he knew only as Scottie who had come around the boarding house and threatened both himself and Emily with a straight razor. He claimed that Scottie made the reference that Emily had ruined his life. Police were never able to identify Scottie.

Crabtree also mentioned a man by the name of Robert Mackie, who was also known as Scotch Bob. This man, he testified used to spend a great deal of time with Emily. Police investigated Mackie and at first believed that he had been in Scotland at the time of the murder, but then they found out that the dates he claimed he had been in Scotland were incorrect. However, for some reason, Police never followed up on this suspect.

Two other witnesses, a Mr. Sharpies and a Mr. Harvey testified that they had seen Emily around midnight on the night of her murder at Kings Cross accompanied by a big man who was not Robert Wood. Police were never able to identify this man either.

In spite of the numerous witnesses and the continuing list of suspects, there was a never-ending stream of theories regarding this murder. One of the most interesting was that it was the work of Jack the Ripper. In this theory, it was alleged that Jack was actually Walter Sickert, a renowned artist of the day. Sickert had been suspected by many of being Jack the Ripper and he lived near Emily's flat and demonstrated a fascination for her murder.

It is true that Sickert was one of many suspected of being Jack the Ripper, but it was never proven. It is also true that Sickert was fascinated with Emily's murder but the primary evidence against him was a series of paintings and sketches showing clothed men sitting near or standing over naked women.

To add fuel to this particular fire, in 2002, crime writer Patricia Cornwell wrote a book that not only accused Sickert of being Jack the Ripper, but she also alleged that he killed Emily Dimmock as well. She claimed that many of his paintings bore an uncanny resemblance to the Ripper crime scenes. Her theories were somewhat discredited when she was accused of having destroyed one of his paintings while trying to obtain DNA to prove he committed the crimes.

Certainly, proving that Walter Sickert was Jack the Ripper and also committed the Camden Town Murder would be a major feather in any investigator's hat. However, the chance that the same person committed both the Ripper murders and killed Emily Dimock is slim. After all, it must be remembered that there was a twenty-year gap between the last certain Ripper murder and the death of the young prostitute. Additionally, while there were some similarities, there were also a number of differences.

Of course, a thorough forensic examination just might reveal some clues that have not been previously revealed. Who know? Only the Shadow!

INDEX

A

Adamson, Carl, 180, 181, 182
Anderson, John, 55
Anna Schneider, 31
Arbuckle, Roscoe "Fatty", 184
Astor Library, 60
Astor, John Jacob, 56
Atlanta Constitution, 117, 119, 134
Atlanta Ripper, 155, 156, 158, 161, 166, 167, 168

B

Battle of Los Angeles, 4
Belson, J. B., 153
Bennett, John, 138
Bertillon, Alphonse, 13
Besumer, Louis, 25, 27, 29, 31
Billy the Kid, 174
Blasier, Ollie, 147, 148
Bloomfield Mortuary, 94
Blue, Monte, 192
Boca, Steve, 40
Brazel, Jesse Wayne, 179
Brooks, Maggie, 158
Brown, Georgia, 161
Brown, Joseph Mackey, 132
Burns, William J., 104

C

Camden Town Murder, 197, 211
Carlson, William, 41
Carr, Bill, 175
Charity Hospital, 30, 31, 34, 35, 40
Clay. Eugene Herbert, 132
Coleman, John William, 78
Conley, Jim, 105, 110, 111, 120
Conrad, Minnie, 153
Cooper, Dr. J. Clark, 66
Cooper, James Fenimore, 55
Cornwell, Patricia, 210
Cortimiglias, Charles, 38
Cortimiglias, Mary, 38
Cortimiglias, Rosie, 38
Cox, W.W. "Bill", 180
Crabtree, John William, 198
Curry, George, 178, 179

D

Darley, N. V., 92
Dean, H. E., 141, 142
Deane-Tanner, William Cunningham. *See* William Desmond Taylor
Dimmock, Emily, 197, 201, 203, 205, 208, 210
DNA, 11, 12, 14, 60, 154, 210
Dobbs, E., 132
Donehoo, Paul, 98
Dorsey, Hugh, 119, 120
Duncan, Mary Ann, 167
Durand, Al, 37

E

Eagle, 200, 203, 205, 207
Edinburgh Courant, 57
Elliot, Lucky, 169
Epps, George, 93, 94, 102, 106
Evans, Edgar, 170
Ewing, Wesley, 66

F

Fall, Albert Bacon, 182

Ferguson, Helen, 94, 123
Ferguson, Ida, 169
Florence, Eva, 168
Fountain, Colonel Albert Jennings, 175
Frank, Leo, 77, 79, 90, 91, 98, 101, 102, 103, 105, 109, 114, 119, 120, 123, 125, 126, 135
Frey, William, 133
Fuller, Eleanor "Nora", 137

G

Gantt, J.M., 92, 97
Garrett, Dudley Poe, 179
Garrett, Pat, 173, 174, 179
Genusa, Frank, 40
Gilder, Roy Van, 74
Gilliland, James, 175
Gillon, Hazel, 186
Gleason, James, 33
Graham, Madge, 146, 147
Great Moon Hoax of 1835, 57

H

H. M. Maple and Company, 178
Hadley, Charles B., 147, 148, 149
Hall, Edward Marshall, 206
Halleck, Fitz-Greene, 56
Hamilton, Ethel May, 185
Harris, H.F., 95
Hawkins, C. B., 142, 145, 148
Hawkins, Mrs. C.B., 144
Henderson, Todd, 167
Herschel, Sir John, 57
Hix, Grace, 90
Holley, Sadie, 165
Hollis, W. T., 106
Holloway, E. L., 112
Hough, Dr. Edgar, 66
Howell, Robert E., 134
Huff, Henry, 166, 167

I

Iowa
  Villisca, 63
Ireland, John Governor, 174
Irving, Washington, 56

J

Jack the Axeman, 21, 26, 31, 44, 45, 52, 75
Jack the Ripper, 17
Jefferies, Alec, 14
Jones, Senator Frank F., 69
Jordano, Frank, 38
Jordano, Iorlando, 38, 39

K

Kelly, Lyn George Jacklin, 72
Kirkwood, Jack, 192
Knights of Mary Phagan, 132
Krone, F. W., 139

L

Laumann, Sarah, 42
Laveau, Marie, 20
Leather Apron. *See* Jack the Ripper
LeBeouf, Joseph, 37
Lee, Newt, 80, 81, 83, 85, 89, 90, 95, 99, 100, 101, 102
Lee, Oliver M., 175
Little Lord Fauntleroy, 151, 154
Locke, Richard Adams, 57
Lohman, Ann Trow. *See* Madame Restell
Louisiana
  DeRidder, 48
  Lake Charles, 49
  New Orleans, 19, 20, 26, 37, 44, 45, 46, 47, 48, 51
Louisana
  Alexandria, 46, 48

Lowe, Harriet, 25, 27, 29, 30, 31

M

MacCowan, Robert, 204
Maggio, Andrew, 23
Maggio, Catherine, 22
Maggio, Jake, 23
Maggio, Joseph, 22
Mansfield, William "Blackie", 71
Matthews, W. M., 106
McLean, Faith, 186, 189
McNeal, Charles, 160
McNeal, Lucinda, 160
McNew, William, 175
Menke, A., 147
Miller, James Brown, 180
Minter, Mary Miles, 190, 191, 192
Moore, Arthur, 63
Moore, Herman, 63
Moore, Josiah, 63
Moore, Mary, 63
Moore, Paul, 63
Moore, Ross, 65
Moore, Sarah, 63
Morris, Judge Newt, 134
Moyer, Sam Moyer, 74
Mrs. Brown, 179
Mrs. Edward Schneider. *See* Anna Schneider
Mullinax, Arthur, 97
Mumfre, Joseph, 45

N

National Pencil Company, 79
New Mexico
   Oro Grande, 179
New Mexico, Roswell, 4
New York Sun, 56
Newman, Norman, 176
Normand, Mabel, 185, 190, 191, 193

O

O'Laughlin Stone Company, 151, 152
Orlando, Giovanni "John", 48
Orlando, Mary, 49
Owens, Alacy, 170

P

Paramount Studios, 187, 194
Payne, Daniel, 57, 59
Peavy, Henry, 187, 193
Peckham, Mary, 64, 65
Pepitone, Mike, 43, 44
Pepitone, Mike Mrs., 45, 46
Phagan, Frances, 78, 94
Phagan, Mary, 77, 80, 81, 83, 90, 91, 94, 95, 96, 97, 98, 99, 100, 101, 102, 106, 109, 111, 118, 119, 121, 128, 132
Phyllis. *See* Emily Dimmock
Poe, Edgar Allen, 53
Popular Restaurant, 138
Powell Lumber Company, 50
Putnam, Mary, 169

Q

Queen of Voodoo. *See* Laveau, Marie
Quinn, Lemmie, 108

R

Reid, Della, 156
Restell, Madame, 58
Rhode, Archie Prentice "Print", 180
Rising Sun, 199, 200, 203
Roan, Leonard S., 120
Roberts, Robert Percival, 200, 205, 206, 208
Robinson, Pearl, 98
Rogers, Mary Cecilia, 53, 56

Rogers, Phoebe, 55
Romano, Joseph, 34, 35
Romano, Mary, 34
Romano, Pauline, 34
Roosevelt, President Theodore, 176
Roosevelt's White House Gunfighters, 176

S

San Francisco Chronicle, 138, 148
Sands, Edward, 193
Scalisi, Frank, 50
Scalisi, Marlena, 49
Scalisi, Mary, 50
Schiambra, Tony, 24
Scotch Bob. *See* Mackie, Robert
Scottie, 208
Sentell, E. L., 97, 98
Sessions, Moultrie McKinney, 132
Sharpe, Emma Lou, 164
Shaw, Bert, 198, 200, 202
Shelby, Charlotte, 192
Sickert, Walter, 209, 211
Slaton, Governor, 130, 132
Smith, William Manning, 118
Spero, Joseph, 47
Spero, Rosa, 46, 47, 48
Start, Charles, 149
Stillinger, Ina, 64
Stillinger, Lena, 64, 67
Stover, Monteen, 106, 107

T

Taylor Thomas, 13
Taylor, William Desmond, 183, 184, 185, 187, 189
Taylor, William Desmond Taylor, 194
Terrell, C.F. Mrs., 97

the Atlanta Journal, 119, 125, 134
The *Georgian*, 118
THE OCCULT CONNECTION, 4
The *Times-Picayune*, 29
Thompson, Gilbert, 13
Times and Commercial Intelligence, 56
Tom Powers, 177
Trice, Rosa, 159

U

Umbsen & Company, 141

V

Vidor, King, 183
Villisca Axe Murders, 63

W

Walker, Mary "Belle", 162
Watts, Addie, 162
Watts, Lizzie, 162
Westcott, William, 207
Whitechapel Murderer. *See* Jack the Ripper
Wilkerson, Detective James, 70
Williams, Pearl, 170
Wise, Bud, 168
Wise, Minnie, 168
Wood, Robert, 199, 200, 202, 203, 204, 206, 207, 208, 209
Woodward, Jimmy, 130

Y

Young, Ruby, 202

Z

Zanca, John, 26

www.ingramcontent.com/pod-product-compliance
Lightning Source LLC
Chambersburg PA
CBHW071905110526
44591CB00011B/1560